HANGING ON OUR OWN BONES

JUDY GRAHN

 Arktoi Books

Book layout by Silvia Gomez & Selena Trager

Library of Congress Cataloging-in-Publication Data

Names: Grahn, Judy, 1940-author.
Title: Hanging on our own bones / Judy Grahn.
Description: First edition. | Pasadena, CA : Arktoi Books, [2017]
Identifiers: LCCN 2017007482 | ISBN 9780989036139 (softcover : acid-free paper)
Classification: LCC PS3557.R226 A6 2017 | DDC 811/.54—dc23
LC record available at https://lccn.loc.gov/2017007482

The National Endowment for the Arts, the Los Angeles County Arts Commission, the
Dwight Stuart Youth Fund, the Max Factor Family Foundation, the Pasadena Tournament
of Roses Foundation, the Pasadena Arts & Culture Commission and the City of Pasadena
Cultural Affairs Division, the City of Los Angeles Department of Cultural Affairs, the
Audrey & Sydney Irmas Charitable Foundation, Sony Pictures Entertainment, Amazon
Literary Partnership, and the Sherwood Foundation partially support Red Hen Press.

First Edition
Published by Arktoi Books
An imprint of Red Hen Press
www.redhen.org

ACKNOWLEDGMENTS

Thanks to Kate Gale and Mark Cull, and the staff of Red Hen Press, and especially my editor Terry Wolverton. I also need to thank my wife, Kris Brandenburger, for her feedback, as well as my friend Dianne Jenett for hers. My gratitude also belongs to those many people who contributed to the shaping and distribution of these poems over the past forty-three years.

CONTENTS

INTRODUCTION
Contemporary Lamentations in Nine Parts

V was sitting in my office wiping tears from her cheeks and eyes; she was one of my older students, very dedicated to women's rights, and I knew she worked as a volunteer in a battered women's shelter. "I just keep thinking about this friend of mine who also works at the shelter," she said.

"Her son was killed last month by the police, for no reason, no reason at all. He had an emotional breakdown, that's all, and he was shouting and holding a knife—not even a big knife, a little knife—I just feel so terrible for her, and so angry."

V's grief and outrage passed over to me, and because I cared so much about her, it was as if I too knew the mother, and the murdered son.

At the same time another student, Anna Knox, was telling me about her struggles to get her schizophrenic mother cared for in the mental health system. Their stories deeply affected me, all the more so as my own mother, now passed, had suffered from schizophrenia. I was also witnessing an upsurge of homelessness in the city, and obviously troubled war vets returning from Iraq and Afghanistan.

Within a few weeks a confluence of emotionally vivid images and stories rose up in me, spilling out in the form of a nine-part poem I called "Mental."

Grief, anger, and a deep collective sense of injustice motivated my poetic mind. Similar confluences had motivated the other poems in this collection as well, though organized around different themes: women as a gender left out of history, or roots of white supremacy in a family dynamic, or the pressing need (and possibility) for individuals to take authority and responsibility for social problems. The poems in this collection are united in these overlapping and related themes as well as in their structure as nine parts of a single thought-feeling.

The seven poems were written over a long period of time, from 1973 to 2016, yet their relationship seems clear. I've wondered how to describe that relationship. The poems are all narrative in form, but interspersed with lines based in rhythm. "We were driving home slow, my lover and I / across the long Bay Bridge, / one February midnight, when midway / over in the far left lane, I saw a strange scene." Yet within the same poem, a section breaks into this quirky verse: "Bless this day oh cat our house / help me be not such a mouse."

The opening stanzas of a poem in this collection may lead us to expect a single voice or point of view, but then a polyvocal chorus or a dialogue appears, as in the poem "Amazon Rising from the Dust," when the "Amazon Chorus" breaks into a glorification of their sex-bonding powers: "Horse my pelvis, horse my thighs, / horse the thunder in my eyes . . ." Time also slips around; a poem may appear to be in either a contemporary or ancient time frame, and then jump into the other, or the future. More peculiarly, they may seem to be telling "my" story, but really they are quite a collectivity of experience; and, while some of this is realistic, some is mythic, as in "Helen you always were / the factory," a portrayal of Helen of Troy as a goddess of work, and workers, and of the beauty, as well as the sweat and blood, of labor. Gender also slides, especially in "Mental," where "Mickey" could be any gender, and the soldier has a beard in one line and is identified ambiguously with the "mother" in other lines.

What holds these poems all together, given these and other differences? Recently I happened on a study of an ancient Greek form of lamentation and found some striking similarities.

What is a lamentation? Lamentation in song and poem, especially by women mourning death in public ways, has widespread history, from Africa to Eurasia, at least, if not over the globe. In ancient Greece, lamentations used a formal poetic structure, utilizing meter, metaphor, and rhyme (Alexiou). Antiphony (argumentative dialogue), refrain, and choral voices are also the stuff of lamentation, as is antithesis, saying the opposite of what one means. The delivery can be both private or public tribute to the deceased and—in the case of violent death—a plea for continuance of, or an end to, the war and/or other oppression. The poetic stanzas were usually sung, and in ancient Greek tradition, always by women. Professional lamenters who applied their art in public were members of certain families for whom lamenting was a hereditary occupation. Nature was usually invoked for beauty and power and to divert the grief to an aesthetic and more positive state.

In addition to honoring individuals, lamentations could be used to mark the collective civilian dead of a war or the devastation of a city, as in the Biblical lamentations on the destruction of Jerusalem in 586 BCE, or long before that, by poets of Sumer lamenting destruction of their cities, Lagash for example. The form was also applied to sorrows surrounding deities, as with the sorrowing of Demeter as she searches for her daughter Persephone, or instructions the goddess Inanna gives to her vizier to mourn and play a hand drum before supplicating the gods for her release from the underworld. Poetic rituals marked the annual agricultural "death" of a harvest god such as Adonis in Southern Europe or Osiris in North Africa.

The biblical book of Lamentations grieves the destruction of Jerusalem by the Babylonians, with the city itself metaphorically imagined as a grieving widow. Later, Christian medieval poets delivered laments in Mary's voice for her crucified son.

Blood is connected to lamentation. In Greece, women scratched their cheeks, and two thousand years earlier in Mesopotamia, instructions for lamentation included the tearing of corners of the lips or eyes, of the breast, and of the vulva to produce a dramatic flow of blood as though even their mouths, eyes and wombs bled grief. Wailing or keening might accompany the song/poem.

A lamentation can also be a communal mourning and have political power, especially to draw attention to and affect affairs of state such as the provoking of endless blood feuds, protesting assassinations, and of course lionizing, critiquing, and even stopping or starting warfare. Centuries ago Greek rulers and lawmakers, wishing to consolidate the powers of kings and states, both economically and through military expansion, forbade the traditional lamenting women to perform their public arts. In the laws of Solon (sixth century BCE) restrictions were placed on lamenting to curb its highly emotional provocation, so for instance both bleeding cheeks and torn clothing were forbidden. While the lamenters continued to be female (Alexiou) the lamenting was restricted and this seems to have been part of a family change to male (only) inheritance, and placing an emphasis on public lamenting of (almost exclusively) male war heroes. Hence a change in lamentation practices marked a change in gender power relations and blood rituals as well.

A lamentation, then, pours out of a poet's heart not only from a deep sense of loss, but also of outrage and justice needed or denied; it takes its own time exploring the emotions and implications, and aims at the possibility of transformation, both individual and collective. It may seek to sound an alarm or name the unnamable, and clearly a certain kind of lamentation has been seen as transgressive against oppressive authority or conditions, toward the goal of possible social change. I have wanted to be transgressive in my poetry, incorporating both real-life conditions and goddess mythology, going directly toward critiquing white supremacy, honoring battered women, exalting the powers of menstruation, conflating all labor with birth imagery, and revealing lateral hostilities among potential allies—all in order to arouse a meaningful social critique. But although these are rational thoughts, each poem originated from a deeply felt grief and sense of outrage. So I submit that the seven poems in this collection can be described as contemporary lamentations, as together they use all of the methods attached to the form: metaphors drawing on the powers of nature, meter, chorus, call and response, polyvocality, repetition, antiphony, antithesis, and invoking grief and/or outrage over conditions involving both humans and deities, and both individuals and collectivities.

I certainly never formally studied lamentations, though in eighth grade the English teacher did have us memorize Samuel Coleridge's *The Rime of the Ancient Mariner* in its entirety—surely this long morbid morality tale imprinted on a thirteen-year-old who wanted to become a poet. Coleridge taught me that a poem can contain many emotions and interactions, including with the supernatural. Other groundwork was laid in my childhood readings of Jeremiah's Lamentations, which portray the destroyed city of Jerusalem as a poverty stricken and socially shamed widow. In the book of Job, various poets have been compiled to tell the story of Job's travails using interwoven narrative, tough as well as lush poetic imagery, and dialogues, as Job and his friends try to decipher the moral lessons behind his suffering. In *The Rime of the Ancient Mariner*, Coleridge took his time in detailing ordeals of guilt and despair as the price of not loving and treasuring all the creatures on earth. Perhaps these could all be understood broadly as forms of lamentation.

Lamentations have a wealth of forms and a few requirements—they must read well out loud, they must address current pressing issues, they must make every attempt to be truthful, and their ultimate value rests on how they impact their readers and listeners. So it follows that a criteria for evaluating or explaining a lamentation must surely include some of the effects it has had on readers and listeners. Toward this end Red Hen Press has provided a portion of their web site to host essays on and testimonials to these poems. These include Margot Gayle Backus persuasively describing "A Woman Is Talking to Death" as a "lesbian invocational elegy;" Joe Moffett placing *The Queen of Swords* in a context of Charles Olson; Delia Fisher and Johanna Dehler exquisitely describing aspects of women's power; a translation of "Mental" into Spanish by Mesha Irizarry, the mother of the murdered young man in section seven, and much more.

The ultimate task of a public lamentation is "to move people." This is more than a description of emotional impact, it's also a geography of the heart, to move people into places of empathy and courage, even action. Many have been moved to perform the poems in this volume, onstage, in bars, in prisons; others have been moved to translate them, or set parts to music, jazz, folk, rock. Often people say they have done this as a response to rape or battery, as response to war, or racism, or other forms of social death. Some of the poems have been smuggled into homophobic countries, or used in classrooms as psychological tools for healing trauma and exclusion. For me personally, they keep me in community.

Elliott Femynye batTzedek has written of reading one of them at Yom Kippur, "as a liturgy of failure and redemption that speaks to the very center of my life." Elliot continues, "This is what it means to live deeply with a poem for twenty years, to have encountered it in so many different parts of your life that its presence is thread through a needle, and everything you do is stitched with it. At the moment that a poet's words become the best words to describe your own reality, the poem becomes sinew, stretching from the poet to you, across time and distance and culture."

Source: Margaret Alexiou. *The Ritual Lament in Greek Tradition*. Lanham: Bowman & Littlefield Publishers, 1992.

A WOMAN IS TALKING TO DEATH (1973)

"A Woman Is Talking to Death," written in 1973, addressed issues raised by all the social change and civil rights movements that impacted my young life, and especially the question of personal responsibility. Even when we do our best to be helpful, it isn't always enough. The poem is a template for the six other nine-part poems that followed it, each of them addressing a portion of the broad-stroked mother poem. As a form, it uses very little myth or older literature, though Cinderella's carriage is discernible on the bridge, as are the "six white horses" of the cowboy dirge, "Streets of Laredo." By and large, this poem is "just the facts" of real events. (The poem was originally published as a sturdy chapbook by the Oakland Women's Press Collective, 1974, and numerous editions and collections thereafter, including online postings. It is included in Honor Moore's Poems from the Women's Movement, 2009; and The Judy Grahn Reader, Aunt Lute Press, 2009.)

ONE

Testimony in trials that never got heard

my lovers teeth are white geese flying above me
my lovers muscles are rope ladders under my hands

we were driving home slow
my lover and I, across the long Bay Bridge,
one February midnight, when midway
over in the far left lane, I saw a strange scene:
one small young man standing by the rail,
and in the lane itself, parked straight across
as if it could stop anything, a large young
man upon a stalled motorcycle, perfectly
relaxed as if he'd stopped at a hamburger stand;
he was wearing a peacoat and levis, and
he had his head back, roaring, you
could almost hear the laugh, it
was so real.

"Look at that fool," I said, "in the
middle of the bridge like that," a very
womanly remark.

Then we heard the meaning of the noise
of metal on a concrete bridge at 50
miles an hour, and the far left lane
filled up with a big car that had a
motorcycle jammed on its front bumper, like
the whole thing would explode, the friction
sparks shot up bright orange for many feet
into the air, and the racket still sets
my teeth on edge.

When the car stopped we stopped parallel
and Wendy headed for the callbox while I
ducked across those six lanes like a mouse
in the bowling alley. "Are you hurt?" I said,
the middle-aged driver had the greyest black face,
"I couldn't stop, I couldn't stop, what happened?"

Then I remembered. "Somebody," I said, "was *on*
the motorcycle." I ran back,
one block? two blocks? the space for walking
on the bridge is maybe 18 inches, whoever
engineered this arrogance, in the dark
stiff wind it seemed I would
be pushed over the rail, would fall down
screaming onto the hard surface of
the bay, but I did not, I found the tall young man
who thought he owned the bridge, now lying on
his stomach, head cradled in his broken arm.

He had glasses on, but somewhere he had lost
most of his levis, where were they?
and his shoes. Two short cuts on his buttocks,
that was the only mark except his thin white
seminal tubes were all strung out behind; no
child left *in* him; and he looked asleep.

I plucked wildly at his wrist, then put it
down; there were two long haired women
holding back the traffic just behind me
with their bare hands, the machines came
down like mad bulls, I was scared, much
more than usual, I felt easily squished
like the earthworms crawling on a busy
sidewalk after the rain; *I wanted to
leave.* And met the driver, walking back.

"The guy is dead." I gripped his hand,
the wind was going to blow us off the bridge.

"Oh my God," he said, "haven't I had enough
trouble in my life?" He raised his head,
and for a second was enraged and yelling,
at the top of the bridge—"I was just driving
home!" His head fell down. "My God, and
now I've killed somebody."

I looked down at my own peacoat and levis,
then over at the dead man's friend, who
was bawling and blubbering, what they would
call hysteria in a woman. "It isn't possible"
he wailed, but it was possible, it was
indeed, accomplished and unfeeling, snoring
in its peacoat, and without its levis on.

He died laughing: that's a fact.

I had a woman waiting for me,
in her car and in the middle of the bridge,
I'm frightened, I said.
I'm afraid, he said, stay with me,
please don't go, stay with me, be
my witness—"No," I said, "I'll be your
witness—later," and I took his name
and number, "but I can't stay with you,
I'm too frightened of the bridge, besides
I have a woman waiting
and no license—
and no tail lights—"
So I left—
as I have left so many of my lovers.

we drove home
shaking, Wendy's face greyer
than any white person's I have ever seen.
maybe he beat his wife, maybe he once
drove taxi, and raped a lover
of mine—how to know these things?
we do each other in, that's a fact.

who will be my witness?
death wastes our time with drunkenness
and depression
death, who keeps us from our
lovers.
he had a woman waiting for him,
I found out when I called the number
days later

"Where is he" she said, "he's disappeared."
"He'll be all right," I said, "*we* could
have hit the guy as easy as anybody, it
wasn't anybody's fault, they'll know that,"
women so often say dumb things like that,
they teach us to be sweet and reassuring,
and say ignorant things, because we dont invent
the crime, the punishment, the bridges

that same week I looked into the mirror
and nobody was there to testify,
how clear, an unemployed queer woman
makes no witness at all,
nobody at all was there for
those two questions: what does
she do, and who is she married to?

I am the woman who stopped on the bridge
and this is the man who was there
our lovers teeth are white geese flying
above us, but we ourselves are
easily squished.

keep the women small and weak
and off the street, and off the
bridges, that's the way, brother
one day I will leave you there,
as I have left you there before,
working for death.

we found out later
what we left him to.
Six big policemen answered the call,
all white, and no child *in* them.
they put the driver up against his car
and beat the hell out of him.
What did you kill that poor kid for?
you mutherfucking n—.
that's a fact.

Death only uses violence
when there is any kind of resistance,
the rest of the time a slow
weardown will do.

They took him to 4 different hospitals
til they got a drunk test report to fit their
case, and held him five days in jail
without a phone call.
how many lovers have we left.

there are as many contradictions to the game,
as there are players.
a woman is talking to death,
though talk is cheap, and life takes a long time
to make
right. He got a cheesy lawyer
who had him cop a plea, 15 to 20
instead of life
Did I say life?

the arrogant young man who thought he
owned the bridge, and fell asleep on it
he died laughing: that's a fact.
the driver sits out his time
off the street somewhere,
does he have the most vacant of
eyes, will he die laughing?

TWO

They don't have to lynch the women anymore

death sits on my doorstep
cleaning his revolver

death cripples my feet and sends me out
to wait for the bus alone,
then comes by driving a taxi.

the woman on our block with 6 young children
has the most vacant of eyes
death sits in her bedroom, loading
his revolver

they don't have to lynch the women
very often anymore, although
they used to—the lord and his men
went through the villages at night, beating &
killing every woman caught
outdoors.
the European witch trials took away
the independent people; two different villages
—after the trials were through that year—
had left in them, each—
one living woman:
one

What were those other women up to? had they
run over someone? stopped on the wrong bridge?
did they have teeth like
any kind of geese, or children
in them?

THREE

This woman is a lesbian be careful

In the military hospital where I worked
as a nurse's aide, the walls of the halls
were lined with howling women
waiting to deliver
or to have some parts removed.
One of the big private rooms contained
the general's wife, who needed
a wart taken off her nose.
we were instructed to give her special attention
not because of her wart or her nose
but because of her husband, the general.

as many women as men die, and that's a fact.

At work there was one friendly patient, already
claimed, a young woman burnt apart with X-ray,
she had long white tubes instead of openings;
rectum, bladder, vagina—I combed her hair, it
was my job, but she took care of me as if
nobody's touch could spoil her.

ho ho death, ho death
have you seen the twinkle in the dead woman's eye?

when you are a nurse's aide
someone suddenly notices you
and yells about the patient's bed,
and tears the sheets apart so you
can do it over, and over
while the patient waits
doubled over in her pain
for you to make the bed *again*
and no one ever looks at you,
only at what you do not do

Here, general, hold this soldier's bed pan
for a moment, hold it for a year—
then we'll promote you to making his bed.
we believe you wouldn't make such messes

if you had to clean up after them.

that's a fantasy.
this woman is a lesbian, be careful.

When I was arrested and being thrown out
of the military, the order went out: dont anybody

speak to this woman, and for those three
long months, almost nobody did;   the dayroom, when
I entered it, fell silent til I had gone; they
were afraid, they knew the wind would blow
them over the rail, the cops would come,
the water would run into their lungs.
Everything I touched
was spoiled. They were my lovers, those
women, but nobody had taught us to swim.
I drowned, I took 3 or 4 others down
when I signed the confession of what we
had done   together.

No one will ever speak to me again.

I read this somewhere; I wasn't there:
in WW II the US army had invented some floating
amphibian tanks, and took them over to
the coast of Europe to unload them,
the landing ships all drawn up in a fleet,
and everybody watching. Each tank had a
crew of 6 and there were 25 tanks.
The first went down the landing planks
and sank, the second, the third, the
fourth, the fifth, the sixth went down
and sank. They weren't supposed
to sink, the engineers had
made a mistake. The crews looked around
wildly for the order to quit,
but none came, and in the sight of
thousands of men, each 6 crewmen
saluted his officers, battened down
his hatch in turn and drove into the
sea, and drowned, until all 25 tanks
were gone. did they have vacant

eyes, die laughing, or what? what
did they talk about, those men,
as the water came in?

was the general their lover?

FOUR

A Mock Interrogation

Have you ever held hands with a woman?

Yes, many times—women about to deliver, women about to
have breasts removed, wombs removed, miscarriages, women
having epileptic fits, having asthma, cancer, women having
breast bone marrow sucked out of them by nervous or in-
different interns, women with heart condition, who were
vomiting, overdosed, depressed, drunk, lonely to the point
of extinction: women who had been run over, beaten up.
deserted. starved. women who had been bitten by rats; and
women who were happy, who were celebrating, who were
dancing with me in large circles or alone, women who were
climbing mountains or up and down walls, or trucks or roofs
and needed a boost up, or I did; women who simply wanted
to hold my hand because they liked me, some women who
wanted to hold my hand because they liked me better than
anyone.

These were many women?

Yes.   many.

What about kissing?   Have you kissed any women?

I have kissed many women.

When was the first woman you kissed with serious feeling?

The first woman ever I kissed was Josie, who I had loved at
such a distance for months. Josie was not only beautiful,
she was tough and handsome too. Josie had black hair and
white teeth and strong brown muscles. Then she dropped
out of school unexplained. When she came back she came
back for one day only, to finish the term, and there was a
child in her. She was all shame, pain, and defiance. Her eyes
were dark as the water under a bridge and no one would
talk to her, they laughed and threw things at her. In the
afternoon I walked across the front of the class and looked
deep into Josie's eyes and I picked up her chin with my
hand, because I loved her, because nothing like her trouble
would ever happen to me, because I hated it that she was
pregnant and unhappy, and an outcast. We were thirteen.

You didn't kiss her?

How does it feel to be thirteen and having a baby?

You didn't actually kiss her?

Not in fact.

You have kissed other women?

Yes many, some of the finest women I know, I have kissed.
women who were lonely, women I didn't know and didn't
want to, but kissed because that was a way to say yes we are
still alive and loveable, though separate, women who
recognized a loneliness in me, women who were hurt, I confess to
kissing the top of a 55 year old woman's head in the snow in

boston, who was hurt more deeply than I have ever been hurt, and I wanted her as a very few people have wanted me—I wanted her and me to own and control and run the city we lived in, to staff the hospital I knew would mistreat her, to drive the transportation system that had betrayed her, to patrol the streets controlling the men who would murder or disfigure or disrupt us, not accidentally with machines, but on purpose, because we are not allowed out on the street alone—

Have you ever committed any indecent acts with women?

Yes, many. I am guilty of allowing suicidal women to die before my eyes or in my ears or under my hands because I thought I could do nothing, I am guilty of leaving a prostitute who held a knife to my friend's throat to keep us from leaving, because we would not sleep with her, we thought she was old and fat and ugly; I am guilty of not loving her who needed me; I regret all the women I have not slept with or comforted, who pulled themselves away from me for lack of something I had not the courage to fight for, for us, our life, our planet, our city, our meat and potatoes, our love. These are indecent acts, lacking courage, lacking a certain fire behind the eyes, which is the symbol, the raised fist, the sharing of resources, the resistance that tells death he will starve for lack of the fat of us, our extra. Yes I have committed acts of indecency with women and most of them were acts of omission. I regret them bitterly.

FIVE

Bless this day oh cat our house

"I was allowed to go

3 places, growing up," she said—
"3 places, no more.
there was a straight line from my house
to school, a straight line from my house
to church, a straight line from my house
to the corner store."
her parents thought something might happen to her.
but nothing   ever   did.

my lovers teeth are white geese flying above me
my lovers muscles are rope ladders under my hands
we are the river of life and fat of the land
death, do you tell me I cannot touch this woman?
if we use each other up
on each other
that's a little bit less for you
a little bit less for you, ho
death, ho ho death.

Bless this day oh cat our house
help me be not such a mouse
death tells the woman to stay home
and then breaks in the window.

I read this somewhere, I wasn't there:
In feudal Europe, if a woman committed adultery
her husband would sometimes tie her
down, catch a mouse and trap it
under a cup on her bare belly, until
it gnawed itself out, now are you
afraid of mice?

SIX

Dressed as I am, a young man once called
me names in Spanish

a woman who talks to death
is a dirty traitor

inside a hamburger joint and
dressed as I am, a young man once called me
names in Spanish
then he called me queer and slugged me.
first I thought the ceiling had fallen down
but there was the counterman making a ham
sandwich, and there was I spread out on his
counter.

For God's sake I said when
I could talk, this guy is beating me up
can't you call the police or something,
can't you stop him? he looked up from
working on his sandwich, which was *my*
sandwich, I had ordered it. He liked
the way I looked. "There's a pay phone
right across the street," he said.

I couldn't listen to the Spanish language
for weeks afterward, without feeling the
most murderous of urges, the simple
association of one thing to another,
so damned simple.

The next day I went to the police station
to become an outraged citizen
Six big policemen stood in the hall,

all white and dressed as they do
they were well pleased with my story, pleased
at what had gotten beat out of me, so
I left them laughing, went home fast
and locked my door.
For several nights I fantasized the scene
again, this time grabbing a chair
and smashing it over the bastard's head,
killing him. I called him a spic, and
killed him. My face healed. his didnt.
no child *in* me.

now when I remember I think:
maybe *he* was Josie's baby.
all the chickens come home to roost,
all of them.

SEVEN

Death and disfiguration

One Christmas eve my lovers and I
we left the bar, driving home slow
there was a woman lying in the snow
by the side of the road. She was wearing
a bathrobe and no shoes, where were
her shoes? she had turned the snow
pink, under her feet. she was an Asian
woman, didnt speak much English, but
she said a taxi driver beat her up
and raped her, throwing her out of his
care.
what on earth was she doing there
on a street she helped to pay for

but doesn't own?
doesn't she know to stay home?

I am a pervert, therefore I've learned
to keep my hands to myself in public
but I was so drunk that night,
I actually did something loving
I took her in my arms, this woman,
until she could breathe right, and
my friends who are perverts too
they touched her too
we all touched her.
"You're going to be all right"
we lied. She started to cry
"I'm 55 years old" she said
and that said everything.

Six big policemen answered the call
no child *in* them.
they seemed afraid to touch her,
then grabbed her like a corpse and heaved her
on their metal stretcher into the van,
crashing and clumsy.
She was more frightened than before.
they were cold and bored.
'don't leave me' she said.
'she'll be all right' they said.
we left, as we have left all of our lovers
as all lovers leave all lovers
much too soon to get the real loving done.

EIGHT

a mock interrogation

Why did you get into the cab with him, dressed as you are?

I wanted to go somewhere.

Did you know what the cab driver might do
if you got into the cab with him?

I just wanted to go somewhere.

How many times did you
get into the cab with him?

I dont remember.

If you dont remember, how do you know it happened to
you?

NINE

Hey you death

ho and ho poor death
our lovers teeth are white geese flying above us
our lovers muscles are rope ladders under our hands
even though no women yet go down to the sea in ships
except in their dreams.

only the arrogant invent a quick and meaningful end
for themselves, of their own choosing.
everyone else knows how very slow it happens
how the woman's existence bleeds out her years
how the child shoots up at ten and is arrested and old
how the man carries a murderous shell within him
and passes it on.

we are the fat of the land, and
we all have our list of casualties

to my lovers I bequeath
the rest of my life

I want nothing left of me for you, ho death
except some fertilizer
for the next batch of us
who do not hold hands with you
who do not embrace you
who try not to work for you
or sacrifice themselves or trust
or believe you, ho ignorant
death, how do you know
we happened to you?

wherever our meat hangs on our own bones
for our own use
your pot is so empty
death, ho death
you shall be poor

HELEN YOU ALWAYS WERE / THE FACTORY (1981)

Wanting to engage actively with mythology, I chose to write of Helen of Troy in a book-length poem, The Queen of Wands, *of which this is the final offering. I noticed that Helen spent the ten-year war her husband waged against her lover's people making a tapestry. During this tumultuous era, Greek armies captured weavers from the North of Africa and enslaved them, selling their cloth to profit themselves. I came to associate Helen's renowned "beauty" with the fruits of people's labor, the love and care we all put into it, the meaning it gives our lives. The poem is spoken by multiple voices, including a narrator, the mythic "Spider Webster."*

ONE

Spider:

Helen you always were
the factory

Though almost wherever you sat placid,
bent at your creative toil,
someone has built a shed around you
with some wheels to oil, some owner
has put you in the shade to weave
or in a great brick box, twelve stories,
twenty, glassed, neonic and with cards
to time your time.
Though he has removed you from your homey
cottage industry, and made you
stranger to your own
productions, though he titles you his worker,
and himself your boss, himself "producer"

Helen you always were
the factory
Helen you always were producer

Though the loom today be made mechanic,
room-sized, vast, metallic, thundering;
though it be electric, electronic,
called a mill—a plant—a complex—
city of industry—

still it is a loom, simply, still just a frame,
a spindle (your great wand) pistons and rods,
heddle bars lifting
so a shuttle can be thrown across the space created

and the new line tapped down into place;
still there is a hot and womblike bucket
somewhere boiling up the stuff of thread
in cauldrons, and some expert fingers dancing
whether of aluminum or flesh; still there is
a pattern
actualized, a spirit caught
in some kind of web
whether it's called a system
or a network or a double breasted
cordless automatic nylon parachute
still it is a web and
still it comes from you
your standing and your wandish
fingers, source, your flash of inspiration,
your support, your faith in it
is still the fateful thread, however it is spun,
of whatever matter made.

And still it is the one true cord,
the umbilical line
unwinding into meaning, transformation,
web of thought and caring and connection.

Just as, Helen you dreamed and weaved it
eons past, just as your seamy fingers
manufactured so much human culture,
all that encloses, sparks
and clothes the nakedness of flesh and
mind and spirit,
Helen, you always were the factory.

TWO

Hannah:

Flames were already eating
at my skirts,
and I heard one of the girls
behind me screaming just how much
burning hurts. I could see the
people gathered on the sidewalk.
Eight stories high
I stood on the ledge
of the Triangle building
and exclaimed out loud.
Then I took my hat
with its white and yellow flowers
and flung it out, and opening
my purse, I scattered the coins
I had earned
to the shocked crowd.
Then, I took Angelina's hand in mine.
I thought we should go down
in style, heads high
as we had been during the strike
to end this kind of fire.
I grabbed Ellie's fingers to my right;
her clothes were smoking
like a cigarette, my little sister,
so serious, seventeen,
actually gave me a clenched smile
just as we leaped, all three
into the concrete sea.
We fell so far.
We're probably falling still.

They say a hundred twenty
thousand workers
marched on our behalf;
they say our eulogy
was delivered in a whisper;
they say our bodies
landed under the earth,
so heavy we became,
so weighted as we spun down;
they say safety conditions changed
after we were killed.
Because we fell so hard
and caused such pain.
Because we fell so far.
We're falling still.

THREE

    Spider:

Helen you always were
the one enticed

The one consigned
to leave your pile of clothing
by the river while you
bathed your beauty
and were stolen. Always
you are the one thrown over
the shoulder, carried off,
forced to enter the car, the plane,
the bed, at swordpoint; lined up,
loaded onto the ships and
shanghaied, tricked

out of your being, shafted,
lifted and held hostage,
taken for a ride.
Always you are the one
forced to sign the bad
contract, forced to work past sundown;
the queen riding the stern
of her once proud ships,
serving two or ten or twenty years
before the mast,
cheated of all pay at last,
and thrashed by the birch rod,
the cat-o'-nine tail wand.

Helen you always were
the coals stoked
and taken from the hearth,
the precious flama
spilled upon the floor
and blamed and blamed
for the uproar
when the whole house
goes up in smoke . . .

FOUR

Nelda:

We were marched to the coast
where the ships waited.
I remember their masts, tossing,
—the pain of loss,
of being lost—
like spikes, through our hearts.

On the passage over
we were stacked like logs
below the deck, our fragile
and our sick
thrown to the fiery sea.

My whole family died.
My husband, my beloved child;
my village, my past life
became a dream.
I barely existed
when I arrived,
for who was "I" to be alive?
Like a lone star
through the blue sky
falling netless
to a new world. What
was new about it was our terror.

But we kept our memories,
we kept our peoplehood, our past.
And oh good god
we stood. We stood in
water to our knees, to plant the
seeds, we stood in ashy fields
and picked the ill-gotten
tobacco and the cotton and
the sugar beets and all the sweet
sweet meats we could never eat.
The sun a dragon.

We spread out
a network to Detroit, Chicago,
Newark and LA, all over the land
for the assemblyline work,

getting blistered in the oil-slick
city streets, scalded in the kitchens
and the laundries, fired in the
fires of hard times. But we did
much more than just survive; we scarred
and healed and sealed and shared and spieled
and blared and smoldered
joining—however knotty it may be—
our memories
our dreaming and our wand-like hands,
to burn together like a great black
brand. A dance of fire.

"Remember dreams, remember Africa,"
we sing, and what we mean
is freedom, wholeness,
that integrity of being
that chooses its own time, its
own kings and queens.

FIVE

   Spider:

Helen you always were
the bag of life

You with your carriage,
the yoni-weaving basket
with the belly-drag,
the well-used pouch,
the cookie jar indefinitely
filled and emptied.

Helen you always were
Santa's fat sack,
full of little worlds
to hang on the great
green tree, so prettily.

Helen you always were the belle
of the ball and the ball
of the bell
with the golden heart,
the egg yolk
of we human folk.

The singing music box
composing magic children
with their sticky
democratic fingers
in your eyes like wands
in water.
The ship's hold stuffed with cargo,
a carving of your image on the bow;
the white sails strung along your arms
like everyday laundry.

Helen you always were
the honeycomb
the honey and the honey jar
kept open by the bear's claw
and words, "we need her,"
and sometimes even, in your nightmare,
the harried wasp who hurries
to lay her hungry eggs
before they hatch inside
and eat her

Helen you always were
the factory
Helen you always were producer

SIX

Nancy:

Do you see the boys lined up
to board the ships
to ride the tanks
around the walls?
The flint-faced fathers
with their scanners
and their maps,
the saplings on the firing
line, woven in the mat
of war, to be rolled out
on any shore
to batter after
every door,
to lie in lifeless lines
across the warehouse floor—
is this the pattern
that I labored and I bore,
the blood for blood, the arms
for arms, the heart
torn out
to hurt some more

And who am I

if it is me
they say
they do it

for?

SEVEN

Spider:

Helen
you always were
the egg laid
by the golden goose,
the full pot, the fat purse,
the best bet, the sure horse
the Christmas rush
the bundle he's about to make;
the gold mine, a house of our own
the ship come in, the next stake,
the nest egg, the big deal, the steal—
the land of opportunity
the lovely lady being
luck and love and lust
and the last chance
for any of us,
the reason that he's living
for, Helen you're always
high card, ace in the hole and
more, the most, the first and best,
the sun
burst
goodness   quenching every thirst
the girl of the golden golden golden

West,
  desire that beats
  in every chest

heart of the sky

and some bizarre
dream substance
we pave streets with
here in America

EIGHT

  Annie Lee:

Oh hell yes! I stand
have stood, will stand;
my feet are killing me!

This tube of lipstick
is *my* wand,
this pencil and this emery board,
this mascara applicator
brushing black sex magic
from a bottle
these long fingernails aflame
with hot red polish, and
these pins, these sharp
spike heels, these chopsticks,
this letter opener
this long handled spoon,
this broom, this vacuum
cleaner tube, this spray can
and this mop,

all these cleaning tools
for sweeping, for undoing knots,
these spools and needles, all
these plugs and slugs and soldering
irons, these switchboards and
earphones and computer boards,
these knitting tools for
putting things together,
these are my wands.

In the parade I'm the one
in bangles and short skirt
twirling the rubber-tipped
baton; this is my umbrella,
and my parasol, my fan,
these are my wands
and oh hell yes I stand

I am who stands
I am also who sits
who greets   who wipes
who notices, who serves,
who takes note
and I am who stoops
who picks and sorts
who cuts and fits
who files and stores
who seals and bonds

and I need my wands
and oh hell yes I stand,
have stood, will stand,
in lines, in queues, in rows,
in blocks, in crowds, in basic
traffic pattern flows.

I have my wands, my hands,
my ways of understanding
and my family strands.

And here in the sunset
is where I like to hear
the singing
of the loom.
The strings of light
like fingers and
the fingers like a
web, dancing. It has
all the meaning
we have made of it.

NINE

Spider:

And still it is a loom, simply,
still just a frame, a spindle,
heddle bars lifting
so a shuttle can be thrown across
the space created
and the new line
tapped down into place;
still there is a hot and womblike bucket
somewhere boiling up the stuff of thread
in cauldrons, and some expert fingers
dancing . . .

Still it is the one true cord,
the umbilical line
unwinding into meaning,

transformation,
web of thought and caring and connection.

Just as, Helen you dreamed and weaved it
eons past, just as your seamy fingers
manufactured so much human culture,
all that encloses, sparks
and clothes the nakedness of flesh and
mind and spirit,

Helen, you always were the factory.
Helen, you always were the factory.
Helen, you always were the factory.
Helen you always were producer.

Helen you always were
who ever is
the weaving tree
and Mother of the people.

DESCENT TO THE ROSES OF A FAMILY (1985)

The false category of "white" people in the U.S. created the concept and social structures of white supremacy, as well as the n-word that helps keep it a terrifying reality. As a Euro-American from a racist family, it's my lifelong moral obligation to do what I can to undo this murderous, oppressive system. Deconstructing what the use of the n-word does within a white family suggests that the psychological dynamic of projection plays a huge role, and therefore change is possible. The n-word itself is volatile, painful for its victims to read, so I am using an alternative spelling, one suggested by Jewlyes Gutierrez, a youthful transgender person, as her way of coping with its effects on her. The spelling is more emotionally accurate, and places the inner, and hidden, meaning of the expression back on the speaker, not the intended target. (This was originally published by Common Lives/Lesbian Lives, Iowa City, 1986, with the title Descent to the Roses of the Family.)

ONE

Last Thanksgiving when our old father,
wrapped in the lap robe I gave him one Christmas,
gathered his family around his knees
to tell us what heritage we had from him—
he said, "The reason the white people are superior
is that the white people are the only human beings"—
and I fell.

I saw each of us falling
into the gall of old habits
my own frightened silence
my father's descent to drunkenness
the whip he makes of his tongue
the lash marks in our skin of memories
the peg of neglect and need we're hanging on
no one ever comes to take us down

Our father of the tender moustache
Our father of the immigrants' bitterness
Our father of the woodcarving hands
Our father of weeping when the kitten died
Our father of whistling beloved songs
Our father of providing steak and doughnuts

Our father of the well-told story
Our father of the embracing T-shirt
Our father of the murderous impulse

Our eyes never leave his face,
our smiles hooking for his approval

(that never arrives).
When we see a child helpless before us
we are likely to blossom into rage,
a stick planted into the dirt of experience.
we turn fury, judge and jury,
our arms fall and rise.
whips shape our tongues.
all we have known
we pass on.

> This is the legacy of the white race
> that I will remember long after my death:
> that it beats its children
> that it blunts itself with alcohol
> that its women suffer from a blight: passivity
> that it carries a gun

TWO

At the family gathering
I notice how the children sit—all of us—
remarkably still,
two generations watch
as battered children will
for any twitch or clue.
Our sister's son the worst,
unable to speak without her
cutting him in two
(after she left home she hated men
for years she told me).
She raised him alone.
He watches her face
the way your son watches you.

Our mother watches the mind inside
her own mind.
She perpetually falls out of time.
She goes to Venus.
At six I became a desperate clown
to keep her here.
I have learned to talk to her
for several sentences in a line
by tugging on her starry wall,
howling down her tunnel.
I still need so to be planted
in her garden dirt. O my brother,
tell me what lives over on the planet Venus
more pressing than our childhood Earth?

As I sometimes do, you treat her
like a loveable imbecile.
Unable to escape the mirror of her face
our sister is outfront cruel.

THREE

Well at least you're a white man
yes at least you've got that
and it gives you something, a word to say
for what you're not—
and that's saying a lot

I was forbidden to say the word
by my mother, who has forbidden herself
to say it, children couldn't say it,
though my father
often said it, twenty times a day at times,
certainly more than he said other words,

"I love you," for instance or
"You did that just right,"
and being a drunk my father is free
to say any words he wants.

Between the two of them,
the father and the mother,
we had a lot of talk about en-grrr
in our family, and then we had
a lot of talk about forbidden.
Because I am trying now to really listen
I notice some of the meanings, hidden.

en-grrr is a black core of action
you don't dare take for yourself
en-grrr is the intense motion
chained up in your chest
en-grrr is the bold center
of the forbidden rose
forbidden begins
with the lips pressed tight together
and the eyes half closed
forbidden to move the hips
shoulders and thighs
forbidden to laugh out loud
forbidden to draw pictures in the air
with the face and hands

forbidden to shout, to talk a great deal
forbidden to whistle
to sing in the street, to exult, to go hallelujah
to bend over in half, laughing
to slap the knee
forbidden to tongue language
in a living form

forbidden to hunker down
to roll the eyes in terror
or mock derision
forbidden to know how to curse
someone all the way down the block
en-grrr is the moving center
in the bright red rose.
Underneath forbidden
is the en-grrr-rose.

FOUR

You tell stories, my brother, how
"The en-grrrs are likely to break in on you whenever they
feel like it," you say. Yet I know factually
this is one of those white, white lies.
Who was always breaking in on you
was our white father.
"He threw your brother at the wall a few times,"
my sister told me.
"If you didn't say the right thing at dinner,
pow—across the mouth," you demonstrated for me once,
the sweeping backhand of parental terrorism.
I see your sweet
red bud of mouth in the childhood photos.

Now you tell me you're afraid of en-grrrs.
What is underneath that lie you tell yourself?
I remember you telling me as we drove around town
how well you know the inside of the jail,
you've been in it three or four times.
"How could that be," I asked, "you've only come
to visit them
three or four times over the years."

"And every time," you said, "Dad insists
I drink with him and then I drink too much
and while I'm driving him home
I'm busted for drunk driving."
Well, at least you're alive, but
free?
You were fifty-three years old my brother
when you told me this—and your father eighty-five.

You were the one pegged for scapegoat in the family.
(Though I was the lesbian, the "black sheep," you call it).
But inside the family you were the one brave
and strong enough to play bad boy
and drunk, the one with dirt
on his hands
so the women could be clean and
patient self-enduring righteous white flowers,
not saying the wrong words,
just too stupid to understand the machinations of
a man's world.
You were the one beaten the most, chastised, stigmatized,
turned over to the cops to teach you
a lesson. No wonder your mouth leaks every kind of hatred,
trying to break through the gate of deaf ears.

Our mother is a white rose
bled down to a ghost.
When I say she is a ghost
I mean she lives on Venus,
mostly, fled there long ago—
Our mother has deaf ears
to what she doesn't want to hear
and this is almost everything.
When I enter my mother I find her center
is a black core

of madness
black as the iris of her eye.
Black as the dried blood at the corner of a
child's mouth, our rosebud mouth
my brother. Black as the blood
soaked into my childhood pillow
of hour on bloody hour my body
howling for attention
through my nose.
our mother is a white rose
bled down to a ghost.

FIVE

The women in our family are considered
stupid. After two days of listening to the men deliver
en-grrr jokes and gun stories,
Indian jokes, queer stories and whore stories I too
am stupid. I don't mention that I'm teaching
college, now. You say that you inherited
Dad's "quickness," and you say
I didn't—I'm more like Mom.
Since Mom, especially in gatherings,
withdraws to silent deafness
(they don't talk to human beings on Venus)
I don't take this as a compliment.
Unable to escape the mirror
I sneer.
I live in fear.

My mother's descent to madness
to stupefication
the blue haze inside the iris of her eyes,
the paleness of her face, the gauze of death

over her emotions, the paralysis.
Her refusal to protect me
her absence, the absence of her expression,
the absence in her person
my terror of the bottomless depths
of the depression in her eyes
my mother's denial of her own wildness, our denial
of her atrocity, of her neglect
of her vindictive punishment.
Our collective belief in her innocence.

The thorn of her absolute will
that runs me through
whenever I enter her center,
unguarded. How she sent him—
a bull to do her roaring.
She sent my father to do the torment
in her stead.

She sent him, she sent my father
to do the torment in her stead.
She, my mother, sent him
(in her descent to absence)
to do the torment
in her stead.

and he put his hands upon me but I did not fear
he put his angry thoughts upon me but I did not fear
and of course I feared
but I did not feel the fear
I did not feel anything at all.

       This is the legacy of the white rose
       that I will remember long after my death:
       that its beaten children beat their children
       that it calls alcohol "spirits"

that its women offer their passivity to their families
like a whip.

SIX

en-grrr is a strong feeling
on its own in the world
en-grrr is a black core of anger
you don't directly dare expose
en-grrr is the forbidden passion
running out of your nose
en-grrr is the electric middle
of the emotional rose
forbidden begins with the heart closed
and the throat clamped shut
forbidden begins with the belly flat and still.
forbidden to spit and to feel
your angry opinion spin free
forbidden to roll, to be large-hearted
and to stand short and bending
as well as straight and tall
forbidden to do more than stand stiff,
to understand,
to fall
to turn face up to the laughing sky
and nearly die
forbidden to cry
to sob on the street, to snuffle
to lie moaning on the dear cruel earth
forbidden to stroke flesh, even our own
forbidden to ken life's ordinary wildness
repression begins with the hips locked up
and the mind closed
en-grrr is a treasure store of your own emotions

forbidden expression
the black wet velvet center
of the paralyzed
rose, stolen from you
from the start.
Under the thumb of forbidden
beats the en-grrr-heart.

I remember our father gambling,
how he failed at gambling;
his broad gestures, his big red nose,
I remember him saying *Be* there! *Be* there!
Be there! as he slapped the cards down.
I remember him being a clown.

Our father of welcoming grins.
Our father of fantastic hopefulness.
Our father of slumped in the doorway.

I remember his face ashen when he
didn't bring a thing home,
not even a silly teddy bear,
when he lost himself in the crap game
of his own decisions.
I remember our father laughing,
his hands drawing pictures in the air,
and crying; and you tell me he kicked
a plate glass window in and was hauled off
more than once to jail.

Well at least
he's a drunkard
yes at least he's got that, at least
our father has passion—
some facsimile. He gets his mind back

when he's sober. At least he's there.
I don't remember our mother crying
or gambling, or singing, or raging.
I remember her lips pressed together
and her hands in a tight vise-hold
on the arms of her madly rocking
rocking chair.
Our mother is controlling
and controlled.

SEVEN

my own descent to depression
the blue haze in my mother's eyes
the bottomless gauze of depression
my descent into the wound of it

my own descent into the blue gauze
of my mother's gaze
the absence of her presence
her absence i filled by
falling into it
my descent into the dull pits
of her pupils
my falling endlessly through the dark
the internal cloud of my mother's own madness.

no one has ever robbed me
and many, yes many have robbed me,
but no has ever robbed me
as this has robbed me
my own recurrent paralysis
the grip of the blue haze
its clutch at my heart

the dying feeling, the not caring
the days on end of it
the weeks, the years left out of themselves
the blue gauze shield that has grown
over my heart
my absence to myself, my deafness,
my absence to love
lifted only by some meanness, some anger
my father's meanness
the whip of his voice
the whip of his voice in my voice
cutting through the dread stillness
of my own descent to Venus

cutting the nothing, shredding,
rousing me at last
to some amount of bleeding, to some feeling,
enough to continue.

For protection my brother
you tell me to get a gun—
we are a family with many guns—
and it is true I am angry.
Yet who would you have me shoot, our old father?
My mother, that she refused to protect
or did not properly care for us?
Should I shoot her madness? his whiskey bottles
endlessly hidden and battled over?
Whose death can give me freedom from
my own frightened silence?
Who can I shoot that can return my childhood to me?
I am afraid of violence against my person.
I am more afraid of going mad, of withdrawing.
I'm most afraid of living with torment all my life.
I'm completely afraid of my own passivity.
Who, besides myself, can I shoot to solve any of this?

EIGHT

What happens when the women abdicate their power,
and let the red rose go
in favor only of the white.
What happens when women let the red rose
of passion go, when they go soldier in a thin
lipped line of disapproval, silence,
hips as still as if the iron belt of chastity
wrapped them still.
As though the burning times took everyone
in Europe with some blood in her, left the rest of us
with ash, ash of what we were.
What happens when women
try to rule by being ruled by others
and by being 'good.'
Our mother is not good. And not an angel.
In fact the times her thorny stick is planted
in the solid dirt she's an entire woman.
Our father is not
bad. And no devil.
In fact without the surge to hit and scrape
he's rather human.
Take away the projection,
take away the battery, the arrogance and the alcohol,
and down would come innocence
woodpile and all.

> this is the legacy of the white rose
> that I will remember long after my death:
> that it hides the dirt under its fingernails
> that it calls fingernail dirt "en-grrr"
> that it thinks it can grow roses without fingernail dirt

Which brings me to the women.
See us three females in the photo—
aren't we quiet? aren't we nice?
Nothing en-grrr in the picture,
unless you count my dike clothes
or the bizarre black and silver light
behind our mother's eyes
(shadow of the planet Venus).

Or my sister's fury,
her refusal to be generous
in the face of neglect.
My mother is a white rose
bled down to a ghost,
and behind the gauze of ghost,
a vision, behind the deafness,
words spoken from another planet, age, rhythm,
behind the madness, splendor of the cosmos, real spirits
and a multitude of lives like multicolored leaves,
unfolding.

NINE

Our mother was warned, my sister said, not to marry him,
"everybody said it." He was a gambler—a drunkard,
a no-good—everybody knew it.
Our parents' early pictures show a raucous bold
couple, certain of themselves and their superiority
over others. My mother believed she could control
his monster—arrogance beyond belief.
My mother believed she shouldn't express anger,
and he graciously

agreed to do it for her.
Our father of no belief.

O brother, I don't want you to be the one
to do my violence
O my brother I can do my own
if there is violence to be done I can be the one to do it
and to choose not to do it.

en-grrr is a black core of creation
you don't directly dare explore
a spirit voice inside your middle ear
the quasar hole
in the American soul
en-grrr is the forbidden impression
boiling at mid-earth
en-grrr is the black hole of unprediction
in the carnivorous rose, a glorious garden
of the unknown and unknowable
the who-knows-what's-going-to-happen-next
en-grrr is the unexplained and inexplicable
the unpredictable, the suddenness
of surrender to anything is possible, the seven
come eleven or the snake eyes in the roll
en-grrr is a handful of cards in the alley
the sweet piercing lyric inside the trombone's growl
the stark desire you have in your heart on a Saturday
afternoon and follow it all over town, until
you meet a beautiful Venus and fall in love with her
one time, and another time she takes you
for a terrible fall
en-grrr is clown spirit walking beside you
or plagues that sweep across continents pruning,
pruning, pruning us one and all
a vision magnetizing your whole life's goal

in the form of a black hole opening before you
en-grrr is my own terror
en-grrr is everything we do not have
whenever we think we have it all
under control.
Under the forbidding/forbidden soul of America
lives the en-grrr-soul.

my own descent to find my violence
a white woman searching her depths
looking for her corruptions, seeking them

Wanted: all my own violences to
come home to me
all my own committed atrocities
to come heap themselves in a shitpile
on my doorstep
a pile of roses of every description.
I might hate some of them
but at least they'll be here with me,
yes at least I'll have that.

I don't want my atrocities pacing the streets
without me
standing in police uniforms
over the bodies of dark-skinned men and women
or shrouded in rags, sores and madness
staggering the streets of Berkeley
and the Upper West Side of Manhattan,
and the wide boulevards of the capitol city,
kicking in windows
to balance with evil the scale for the sinless:
the nice polite determinedly "cancer free"
hands on the nice
polite wheat sandwiches

with not too many calories
and not too much insecticide
and not too much MSG
and a neutral colored rose—just one—
in a glass
on the table

    O my brother
    our family's descent
    to find its roses
    the despair of our denial, our roselessness
    the secret of dirt and what grows of it
    the peg of need we're hanging on . . .

AMAZON RISING FROM THE DUST (1986)

"Amazon Rising from the Dust" is the fourth act of a book-length poem, The Queen of Swords *(Beacon Press, 1987). The plot is of Helen of Troy, "most beautiful woman" in ancient Greece, who chose to leave her husband for a lover, triggering a war that devastated the lover's homeland, Troy. In* The Queen of Swords, *Helen is reborn as wife of an upper middleclass scientist, who goes on a mysterious transformational journey to a 1960s-style lesbian bar that is an "underworld." There, she is confronted by dykes who take the form variously of crows, judges, or in this act, Amazon, i.e. women, warriors. As the scene opens, Helen is sweeping the bar floor when she spots a strange lump moving on the floor.*

ONE

Helen
> What dreadful thing is lying there
> as though growing from the floor?

> > (*Corpse of Pen gradually rises from the floor. She looks like a
> > 3,000-year-old corpse, yet underneath the torn flesh, rotten garments,
> > and protruding bones, Pen is actually quite handsome and would be
> > appealing to Helen if she were an entire being.*)

Pen
> I am not graceful in this first movement.

Helen
> You—who are you?

Pen
> I have been the Amazon
> in the dust.
> From dust all things arise.
> I'm a little awkward getting up.

Helen
> Don't bother, then.
> Just sit where you are,
> at least until you have your face on.
> You look like a pile of bones
> from some garbage pit.

Pen (sarcastically, and rising anyway)
> Thanks a lot.
> The last time we met
> was during the great war.

Helen

    The First World War?

Pen

    Not that one,
    the earliest one, the war at Troy
    three thousand years ago.
    You had arrived from Sparta with
    your lover Paris.
    Then your husband and his brother
    took their whole world to war to force
    you back, stripped of your
    protectors, stripped of your freedom, stripped
    finally of your life. Just the day before
    we Amazons arrived, they had killed Hector,
    Troy's best warrior, next to me of course.

Helen

    And who did you say you were?

Pen

    Penthesilea, Amazon Queen, who went once
    to war to save Queen Helen (that was you).
    "Able to make men mourn" my name signifies,
    supreme Amazon speeding to the neediness of Troy,
    leader of twelve good warrior maidens,
    battle-scarred
    and with fierce reputation. We were the last
    hope that queenly Troy could keep intact
    the power of women and the greatest beauty in the world.

        (Crow Dikes begin entering one by one; they lounge
        around the bar casually; then as Pen and Helen speak
        they act out battle scenes; they are Amazon Warriors
        though some take the parts of male Greek warriors in the fray.)

TWO

Helen (gasping)
> I remember that day.
> The sky was a sheet of crystal
> and the wind was still.
> I ran to see your arrival
> from my windowsill.
> You were like Artemis to us,
> you arrow-carrying bear-dikes.
> I could tell how Hector
> and the other men had learnt
> some of their skill from you,
> and then too, what can confuse
> a man more than a naked female
> breast with a bloody ax behind it?

Pen
> You and I met before the fight.
> I rode into the hall
> on the great long-legged stride
> my mother prized me for.
>
> You turned almost at once
> to look me up and down.
> My cheeks burned with pride
> though inside
> I felt more like a clown.

Helen
> The Amazons were coming!
> To fight on our side!
> We women were electrified.
> You looked strange to us
> but exhilarating.
> I was especially electrified by you.

Pen

> I knew it too, that moment
> at least, when our eyes met across the room.
> I was your last battle ax
> and you threw it.

Helen

> By then, with the war in its tenth year,
> I don't think I cared much
> whether I stayed with Paris
> or my husband won and took me home.
> You put up the hardest fight they ever saw,
> carved their gullets and split their craws,
> set them mewling in their own fear,
> pinned to the ground with their own spears.
> I had never seen men die of terror.

Pen

> You flew into a cloud of dust, Helen,
> you withdrew.
> We didn't know what slavery of your beauty
> stood on the other side of my downfall.

THREE

Helen

> I remember that day.
> During the fight
> some of us thought
> we should run outside
> to help you, stand beside
> with shield and mace and other weapons.
> Someone reminded us,
> you trained all your life

for this—we are different,
built to carry a different burden,
stand in a different place.

Pen

I don't know how you are or are not built.
I know you were watching when Achilles killed me.
I know it affected you horribly.

Helen

I wanted to turn my face
and couldn't.
No one imagined
you could ever be beaten,
let alone raped
and dragged around like a dishrag.
Everything fractured then
as the sword clubbed and then went in,
not just the ribs and skull,
the full picture went to pieces, I saw the world
break like a dropped egg.

Pen

Helen your beauty
and your godlike features
cracked like shell
after my own cracking face
and graceless fall.
Oh god Helen, we lost the war;
we lost each other in the war.
I was your tooth
and they pulled it.
I was your dagger
and they tore it
from your hand.

Amazon Chorus
> She was your voice
> and they slit your throat;
> she was your breath
> caught like a duck in a gill net.

Helen
> I stood with all
> the women on the wall, watching,
> hands clutching as you lay on the sand
> blood-drained and stiffening.

Pen
> I was your arrow
> against the foe
> I was your backbone
> bent low
> oh lady of sorrow
> I was your bow.

FOUR

Amazon Chorus
> Helen, your arrow—
> where is it?
> Is it hidden in your pocket?
> Is it long like a rocket,
> or is it round as a locket?
> Is it a bee sting?
> Is it stored in a quiver,
> or under your disgust for slimy things?
> Helen—your arrow,
> do you have it?

Helen

> How horrible that this happened to you,
> how horrible what they did to you.

Pen

> They did it to you, too.
> We have to move through memory
> as the wind sifts through dust, examining
> everything for clues.
> My corpse self was crow-eaten
> and discarded, my power stolen.
> I have to move through that scene to another,
> to the dream remembered,
> a dream of wild horses
> of women's fingers tangled in the manes,
> and tangled with each other,
> in a dream of what we do with horses
> when we do it all together,
> when we do it with one motive.

FIVE

Helen

> Oh yes, I'd rather talk of horses.
> At home I have a shelf of lovely glass horses.
> And I've heard of Amazons with horses.
> I've heard you do the most
> amazing things with horses.

Amazon Chorus

> Horse my pelvis, horse my thighs,
> horse the thunder in my eyes . . .

Helen
> What *do* you do with horses?

Amazon Chorus
> As for what we do with horses
> it's none of your business,
> it's none of your knowing
> what rides we mounted
> what circles rode, what songs shouted.
> It's not for your understanding
> what fires we kindled
> in autumn darkness,
> what flames we handled
> when the moon was
> breathless.
>> As for what
> we did in tandem
> it was the bonding of warriors,
> as for what we did of ritual,
> it was what you now call: actual.
> As for what we learned in shadows
> it's not of your fathom,
> it's deep as molasses
> or a parade of motorcycles,
>
> As for what we do with horses
> we ride them like forces,
> as for what we do with forces,
> we tug them in closer.
> As for what we do with borders
> we cross and uncross them,
> as for what we do with curses,
> we put them in purses
> and fling them to blazes.

As for what we do with horses
we fondle their noses
we drape them in roses
and race them on courses,
it's a great-hearted outpouring
with the whole crowd cheering,
it's not for the artless,
it's how their hoofbeats whisper up
to us, "Destiny, destiny, destiny . . .
rides on solidarity."

As for what we do with horses,
it's the rush of our great trying,
it's the tension of our lunging
it's the love of promising
it's the flesh imagining itself flying
it's the flash of light before thundering,
it's the dark ring of opening,
it's the way we have of living
in the dust of the wind.

Helen
　　That's not anything I've ever done with horses.

SIX

Pen
　　After the fall of women's power,
　　in the dust whirl of dream
　　I lay for centuries hardly moving,
　　paralyzed,
　　recalling only the last act, the rape
　　that Achilles bent to vent himself on me.
　　I thought I would never be free of it,

until at last I began to live again,
and again, to hang at the corner of the ceiling
and recall who I had been.
I saw myself a Roman soldier on the march,
saw myself a Viking on the Normandy coast,
I saw myself a tender-hearted soldier
in the First World War.
Saw myself at last reborn
in my own killer's form.

Helen

You have lived over and over
in the bodies of men?

Pen

When he took our Amazon strength
to be his own he became a soldier; women
such as you and I hung high on a peg, burning.

Helen

Like Joan of Arc! Hung on a stake!

Pen

Then down to the scorpion ground. I have been down
to the bottom of the ditch;
I have been down overcome by my own corpse-stench.
If you could just join forces with me now
you would find the awesome power of nothing
you've been looking for.

Helen

I don't want awesome nothing
and I don't want dust,
I certainly can't join forces
with you, I'm not
part of your war.

Pen
    My war?

Helen
    I stood on the ramparts of the wall,
    while men on the inside warred
    with men on the outside,
    and you manlike Amazons
    mixed it up with the worst of them.
    I stood on the wall; I fled on the stair;
    I have no part of war.
    I live in a glass house, with glass horses;
    I hardly ever come face to face with my own forces.

SEVEN

Amazon Chorus
    Helen, the nature of your strength,
    what is it?

Helen
    Everything I have or am
    I give to men now,
    they fought and won it,
    isn't that correct?
    Besides, they are so strong,
    and losers mushy-chested
    and contemptible.

Amazon Chorus
    Strong, there are so many kinds
    of strong. Men are steadfast
    in what they want,
    that is one.

Amazon strength
lives in the wind, a dance of transformation.

Helen
And Helen's strength, what is it?
Is it the strength of love?

Amazon Chorus
Helen, your strength
is in your memory.

Helen
And is my memory my mother?
What are my memories?

Amazon Chorus
Memory is the mother of truth;
and truth is the mother of beauty;
and beauty is the real mother
of real science.

Pen
Helen. I was your tooth,
and it rotted.
I was your knife and you dropped it
from your hand.
I have endured every humiliation of the battle-lost,
the war-torn. I have sometimes wished not to be born.
I have been called every vile name,
and worst of all, you have seen,
and feared, and scorned, and shunned me.
But names are only identity games, and suffering ends
in toughness or death, what I have never been
is a slave, only the side that lost the war.
Yet without me as the dagger by your side,
slave is quite a bit of what you are.

Helen

> Oh you go on so long,
> and you're so wrong.
> I'm not a slave—
> I'm just well-behaved.
> I live in a nice glass house with glass bells—
> I've been a cherished, petted child—
> lucky person, lucky life—

Amazon Chorus

> Helen, your horses,
> what are they?
> Can you ride them
> or do you hide them?
> Helen—your horses,
> do they lead you,
> or follow?
> Are you keeping them,
> in what meadow?

EIGHT

Pen

> My memory is a long one,
> it gives me no rest.
> Though you recoil from me now
> dressed in my blood and dirt,
> and with my wounded breast—
> is my sack of being
> too leaky for your good taste?
> Still, I'll give you advice
> and of what I have—the best . . .

You say you stand
on the wall, apart, yet
everywhere there's a war
there you are, beautiful, desired
and right in the middle of it.
So I know you're a player,
whether or not you admit it.
This is what I know, Helen,
of the nature of war,
if you stay in battle long enough
you'll find you carry every arm,
do every harm
in every heart
of every storm.
No horse you own remains unridden,
no hand you hold remains unplayed.

Helen

And what of love in all this talk of death?
And what of my high hopes?
And my force? What is it? Is it politics?
Is it science?
What is it really can rise from dust?

Amazon Chorus

Helen, your forces
are in the beauty of your memory,
do you remember?
Can you ride them like horses?

Helen

What is my science?

Amazon Chorus

Your science is in the memory of your beauty.

Helen
> How can I re-form from simple dust
> to remember myself, how can I ever understand
> the nature of my beauty?

Amazon Chorus
> Under the mask of Helen smiling
> lies the Foe,
> under the mask of the Foe
> lies a dead Amazon,
> under the mask of the fallen Amazon
> lies Helen, sleeping.
> Under the mask of Helen sleeping
> lies the lady of the underworld
> birthing fury,
> and under the fury
> stands the bull god,
> wild-eyed, waiting
> for his sacrifice.

NINE

Helen
> I remember, I remember, I remember—
> the sky *is* a sheet of crystal on a day like this
> and I remember the whole war now,
> and later my own crashing fall
> and loss of power.
> What a splash I made!
> What powers I had! What sciences!
> Healing—predicting, even controlling weather.
> Yet after that war
> I was no longer one superior
> focal point of light, like Venus.

I was scattered everywhere,
my villages burned to underground,
the old folks going down
on the forced marches,
after the teachers and the intellectuals
spewed their own blood along the fences,
while the women huddled in whore camps
and everyone ate napalm rations,
our young men clubbed in the police stations,
our children turned to strangers
in the boarding schools of force-fed reculturation,
after the bombs, after the secret warehouse torture,
after the famine and the relocation,
after the war . . .

Pen

I became your fallen warrior eating dust,
my lips flattened in it,
while dogs ripped
at my skin coat the way a man, a soldier
raped my corpse between the legs, and called it
love or lust or even by its better name,
conquest, trying to do the sorcery of
soul-theft.

Helen

I became a cloud, forgetful,
fearful and unpredictable.
Now how can I ever gather myself together again?
Are you one of my forces?
And you—who are you?
You're more blown apart
than I am. I expected a glorious
Amazon, not a blood-dripping corpse.

Pen (kneeling)
   Oh I know I offend you
   with my leaking chest
   and bitter mouth,
   my messages of hard reality,
   but Helen, reach to touch me,
   touch my fingers—dust we always have
   to turn to;
   touch is all we have to give
   each other, while we're here.

   Tangle fingers with me now
   so you can remember who you are,
   and I can live on earth again.

         (*They touch fingers; Helen wipes hers on her shirt, then reaches out
         for Pen's hand, then clutches her, then recoils.*)

Helen (thoughtfully and with mixed emotions)
   Now another woman's blood is on my hands.

         (*All the Amazons become Crow Dikes who stamp their feet, too, and
         howl and whoop. Helen recoils again.*)

WOMEN ARE TIRED OF THE WAYS MEN BLEED (2003)

A lamentation can critique, and also offer positive solutions to a social problem. This poem was written especially for some of my students, and also inspired by research I have done on the creative powers of menstruation. Various sections address "blood rituals," defined as domestic violence, militarism, and destructive, rampant industrialization—differentiated from conscious living, caring parenting, while honoring more peaceful "blood" of earth's beings, and restoring women to power and place in human culture. (Written in 2003, published as a chapbook by St. Mark's Poetry Project, 2015.)

ONE

"I know it's irrational," he said
"but after the Loma Prieta earthquake
I sat up in bed with my pistol
loaded and cocked."

imagine a war
of "shoot the sea—
prevent tsunamis"

imagine if war were seen
as dysfunctional behavior
like child abuse or the many problems
in families, and say, if we wouldn't shoot
our mothers and fathers
even when they terrify or mortally wound us
why would we drop bombs upon
the possibly not even dysfunctional strangers?

imagine if war were seen as just as
vengeful as any vengeful practices,
like, say, after the hurricane we lock up
everything that flies for having brought
the bad wind.
or we blow up the houses of those related
to those supportive of those who live with the drivers
who cause automotive accidents

imagine it's ok
to know humanity
as we might know our dopey, dangerous, loveable
amazingly adaptable and talented family
even those whose love we continue seeking
even those we have tortured or neglected

even those who have hurt us, who oppose us
even those mysterious as water

imagine it's ok
to know the earth
exactly as a person.
imagine Armageddon
already happened
now we're into
reconstruction.
imagine a god named
it's ok.

TWO

every generation has its war.
every war comes home

One son came back from the army
to his new marriage.
"Something is wrong, this isn't
working," he said to his Mom,
"I can't control her, she won't
obey me." "Why must you control
her?" asked the Mom.
"Because—I am like the sergeant,
she is like the recruit, right? This is how
they treated me, and if I
could submit so can she . . ."
"Marriage is not the Army," said the Mom.
"Marriage is roots and leaves
who hold each other equally."

That son listened but no one talked
to the boy who returned from the army
and put a grenade into his bride's mouth
after forcing her to kneel, as they learned
the lesson together:
some wounds are of the heart
some teaching is wounding
some wounds never heal.

Women are tired of the ways men bleed.

THREE

The Vampires of Empire

> *just as*
> *—as the Kogi have told us*
> *gold is the blood of the Earth—*
> *oil is the blood of the Mother*

the Mother's rule
is blood for blood
you eat, you pay

we drink her blood
to fuel our lives
our rule is *glug glug glug*
we're free, we say

if we can't have more than our
more-than-our-share
we call it a crisis
and go to war

we pay the price
an addict pays
if oil costs the blood
of three thousand soldiers
we don't care
if it costs the blood
of forty thousand civilians
we don't care
if it costs the blood
of thirty-five thousand traffic deaths
we don't care

we are the vampires of empire
we can eat cherries in winter
we can fly anywhere
everything we do begins with petroleum
yum yum yum

what did we do this year?
we drank, drank
the blood of the Mother
burp burp burp
we burned, burned
the blood of the Mother

rumrumrum
we drove round
in carriages,
as fast and as far as we could
slurp slurp slurp

the bitter syrup, so
free—we are free
we live in a sea
of burning blood

we can drive anywhere
don't need roads
the earth is our road
our rule is *lug lug lug*

we love our carriages
roomy, safe, we carry homes
and offices with us
pretend our trailer
is a wickiup
make a procession of carry-out,
pick-up
go go drink drink burn burn

where are we going?
what is the purpose of the trip?
we don't care
we love the sensation of getting there
salty illusion of being free
we are the vampires of empire

we go wherever our addiction takes us

the Mother doesn't care either
doesn't intercede
You Eat You Pay she says
and all natural history confirms
she means it.

FOUR

Can hearts be at peace
when marriage and war
become identical experiences?

Women are tired of the ways men bleed
by breaking open
other people's veins.
firemen are brave souls
policemen are brave souls
soldiers are brave souls
and housewives
housewives are brave souls
let us respect the bravery
of housewives

during the Vietnam War
and during the Iraq War,
in the U.S. more housewives and girlfriends,
more brides and mothers
died at the hands of angry husbands and boyfriends
than U.S. soldiers died *in* the Vietnam War or *in*
the Iraq War.
These have been violent periods
for soldiers, housewives and girlfriends.
I don't mean to disrespect soldiers
for their sacrifices
I mean let's honor housewives
as soldiers
in the evolution
of marriage   embedded
in the evolution of war
as the primary initiation rite
for sons, for husbands, for fathers

war is a kind of marriage

Marriage, for many women, is a kind of war

saying "I do" enlistment for
the most dangerous duty, the frontlines
of the husband-centered family
the frontlines of punching bag duty
"honey wontcha be my punching bag"
wontcha catch his emotions
with your face
wontcha let him twist his feelings
around your neck
wontcha put your body between his
expressions of rage
and the children

Do the brides know, like soldiers, do they think about the odds
the way soldiers talk in the training barracks,
what they say packed together in the truck beds on the way to the front?
Do they say to their friend at the bridal shower,
"I might not come back from this."
Do they say to their families, "Send me your love and your courage,
let me always come home when I need to, and don't forget to
put a white cross on the road.
don't forget to put a white cross in front of the house,
don't forget to put a white cross somewhere if I—
if I don't live through this marriage."
Do they whisper to the bridesmaids, "I don't really know him,
what is the family history of violence, what does his
mother say about her life
secretly, to herself?"

Do the bridesmaids answer, "You might not get
through this, he might turn on you the second year
(as happened to J.),
after the first child he might kick you in the stomach
(as happened to V., as happened to M.),
during the pregnancy, he might break your nose the first time

you say no to anything (as happened to D., as happened to R.),
he might never allow you to leave him,
stalking you for years (as happened to L., as happened to N.)."
Does she look in the mirror at the dress fitting,
say to the woman pinning her hem,
"What does he know about himself
that he keeps secret?
What does he not yet
know about himself
that he will learn after he reads
my body as a book?
after he writes on me
the script of his emotions?"

FIVE

Let's make statues of brave, dead brides
and wives who persisted with the marriage
despite wounds and disabilities
despite death threats and knowing other casualties
who stayed patient and frantic,
frantic and patient
abandoned by authorities, priests and preachers,
rabbis, bosses and best friends,
families who would not take them back
mothers-in-law who refused to believe them
authorities who just never showed up.

no marine buddies coming to rescue

Isn't she like an unarmed policeman,
"I stayed to protect the children,
I stayed for the sake of the family."
isn't she like a fireman?

walking steadily upstairs to the flames of rage
in the collapsing architecture of the marriage
"I stayed for the sake of the children, I thought he would
kill them if I left, I thought they needed a father, any kind of father."
isn't she a warrior
guarding the family, guarding the household,
guarding his fatherness with the cells of her body
the brave bride armed only with 911 calls
answered late, unanswered
her screams of terror
the police outside in their car saying,
"Hey, it's a war in there.
we would go in, but what's the use?
She'll only go back to him
to get beaten and beaten again"

as though the medic on the battlefield says:
"Hey, it's a war out here.
what's the use of taking this soldier in,
he'll only go back into battle
he's only going to be shot again and again"

let us raise up walls
walls in every city
and a big wall in Washington,
walls with names and names and names

great red walls for the blood of these soldiers
Precious.   Sacred.   Grieved.

"Our beloved sister, mother, and daughter
she died bravely in the line of duty
to family and country
to marriage and to the evolution
of the patriarchy

we thank her for her sacrifice
we honor her courage
we miss her presence
may her heart be at peace."

*Can hearts be at peace
when marriage and war
become identical experiences?*

SIX

All blood is menstrual blood

Images of blood are all around us, everywhere
in our modern urbanized society blood is
depicted, spoken of, displayed:

The blood of wound, of death and to a tiny extent
birth, is part of daily viewing in television
and films; we are completely familiar
with the bloodlines of kinship, and with the blood
of violence, of murder and vengeance, of sacrifice,
suffering, and of IV drug users; the blood
of warning, of wounding, of threat; the danger
attached to the blood of AIDS; the blood of life, of
transfusions, of redemption; the blood of Christ;
the blood of martyrdom, of St. Sebastian, of the prize
fighter depicted in the movies. Blood is
genealogy in bloodlines, family blood,
the blood that is thicker
than water.

Blood is in name and in common
expression, in the blood of the lamb, in the blood

of blood, sweat and tears, in the blood of the Sangre
de Cristo Mountains, in the blood of blood brothers,
the blood of the stigmata, the blood on the moon,
the blood that cannot be squeezed from turnips,
the blood dripping from the mouth of the vampire,
the bloodstain on Lady Macbeth's hands, the blood
gurgling down the shower drain in horror films.

Real blood is everywhere in our society, Saturday-
night blood, drive-by-shooting blood, the blood he was
covered in after he was shot, or stabbed
or blown up; the pencil-thin line like a necklace
across her throat, the great spread of it when she was
chopped up, the bloody nose, the bleeding ulcer,
the sting of hemorrhoids, the blood on the surgeon's
gown and the butcher's apron, the many rivers of
battle and massacre that have run with blood,
the battlefield soaked, the sand reddened,
the blood on the child's ear and the wife's
mouth and the young man's cheek.

In the cities the gutters are streaming
and sidewalks pooled and car seats puddled and
emergency rooms smeared and police clubs stained.

When gangster John Dillinger's body fell on the street
shot by the FBI and spouting
from numerous holes
passersby instantly leaped as though
to a holy stream, to dip
a handkerchief, newspaper, even
a sleeve into the blood of his wounds, to take
a bit home with them.

Blood is magic
Blood is holy
And wholly riveting of our attention.

Menstrual blood is the only source of blood
that is not traumatically induced.
Yet in modern society, this is the most
hidden blood, the one rarely spoken of
and almost never seen
except privately by women, who shut themselves
in little rooms to quickly and perhaps disgustedly
change their pads and tampons,
wrapping the bloodied cotton so it won't be seen
by others, wrinkling their faces at the odor,
flushing or hiding the evidence away.
Blood is everywhere
and yet the one
the only
the single name
it has not had publicly
for many centuries
is menstrual blood.

Menstrual blood, like water
just flows.
Its fountain existed
long before knives or flint.
Menstruation
is the original source of blood.
Menstrual is blood's secret name.

SEVEN

All blood is menstrual blood.
all praises to:

The blood of creation.
The blood of peace.
The blood of new beginning.
The blood of zero population growth.
The blood of "I don't *have* to go to work today."
The blood of meditative space.
The blood of the first covenant.
The blood of the first paint.
The blood of the first lipstick.
The blood of the first hair color.
The blood of the first cave art.
The blood of the first calendar.
The blood of the first Sabbath.
The blood of the first procession.

The blood of the first food.
      The blood of the first Communion.
      The blood of the first Word.

the blood of the red corn mother
the blood of the red carrot mother
the blood of the red wheat mother
the blood of the red rice mother
the blood of the red millet mother
the blood of the red beer mother
the blood of the red grape mother
the blood of the red wine mother
the blood of the red turmeric mother
the blood of the red yam mother
the blood of the maple tree mother
the blood of the red clay mother
the blood of the red saffron mother
the blood of the red apple mother
the blood of the red pomegranate mother
the blood of the red ochre mother

the blood of the red chocolate mother
the blood of the red coffee mother
the blood of the red pepper mother
the blood of the red pandanus mother
the blood of the red stone mother
the blood of the bleeding tree mother
the blood of the menstruating river mother
the blood of the menstruating volcano mother
the blood of the menstruating moon mother
the blood of the menstruating earth mother
the blood of the menstruating cosmos mother

If I had a bowl
of menstrual blood
I'd take it outside
and give it a
long,
long,
bloody,
bloody,
peaceful,
peaceful,

parade.

EIGHT

Mothers, fathers, clasp the children, tie them to your breast
and beam like flashlights, hold the children praise them with buckets
of raspberries, shiny as jelly, give them you.
Show them they are green-worthy as grass in rain, lofty as kite-flying by
the Bay,
sharp as sunrise after an ice-storm. Grasp them, study their eyes,
talk to them like kittens.

Tell them they have the sturdy grace of deer, communal peace of stones, generosity
of the sea, able, able, capable and ready. Tell them they can learn to be happy
no matter what else is true.
Mothers-fathers grip the children with bearpaws of glee, press them to your hearts,
sing high into their precious ears, drip strawberry down through their lives,
tell the sons they are ships *and* shores, tell the daughters they are mountains
and towns that will thrive a hundred years, say the world is sending them a ticket,
they just need to find the train that's theirs.

Oh winds of change, gather the wounded
boys and girls of all rages
into your giant arms, blow brotherly breath
between their fierce sad eyes, unclench their wish
for motherly porridge, pour fatherly tears
of crooning through their bliss-hungry lips
and tell them this one truth:
when we find or make that motherplace
our vessels heal, contain no leaks
and all around us love pours in, red cells pulse
burning away bleakness
red cells flash as curious pretty fishes
spelling the words
"this is my darling life, and this is enough"

NINE

imagine it's ok if war were understood
as periodic national bleeding
necessary to bring about change
part of the cyclic nature of our humanity

why does this period have to be accomplished
with devastated countrysides, irredeemable murders,
wrecked cities and families enraged with other
families for generations?

All to feed the need
archaic to our beings
of our throbbing vampire heart.
what if I told you every major national u.s. bloodshed
arrives in a twenty-eight-year period pattern
just exactly like a gigantic menstruation
only made of shattered limbs, mashed children, heartbleeding
parents, a 10 to 1 ratio of civilians to soldiers killed,
and what if this made you mad because
you imagine *menstruation*
is a subject so lacking in honor
(compared to war)
but being honest and honorable,
you follow my advice
subtracting 28 from the date beginning Sept 11
two thousand and one, to 1973, and 1945 and so on
until you too see the pattern. When we again look at each other
do you think we will see anything the least little bit
—sensible, justifiable, rational, honorable—
about war that isn't far more true about menstruation?

imagine if we knew our vampire hearts
would drink any blood offered, even the blood of peace?

Imagine if we undertook the bleeding consciously
offering the earth's many peaceful bloods
with intent to omit violence, celebrating
blood of life, and caring, and connection,
bitter blood of vengeance converted into sweet blood
of it's ok to love
the cosmos and its patterns
as we pretend not to notice how eagerly
the fiery vampire tongue slips out of us
to drink and drink the red elixir
cedar vinegar cinnamon honeypot saffron

until how soon we have lost interest in war and woundedness
imagine unfamiliar satisfactions setting in
filling our breasts with maple syrup swellings

constructing rituals that account for violent emotions
discharging them appropriately, artfully,
dominating ourselves but not each other,
leaving children and trees in peace
instead of pieces
filling our hearts with luscious feelings,
and no vengeance to exact
on anyone, not even the Mother, not even God.

MENTAL (2005)

The explosion of homelessness, especially homeless vets, and runaway police vio-lence in the U.S. in the decades following the 1970s, coupled with my own will-ingness to address mental illness in my family, led to this poem, written in 2005. However, the most pressing impetus driving it is the ongoing ill treatment and overt murder of African-American people, especially young men, as well as those people termed "mentally ill." So, while it may read as autobiographical, very few lines are about me or my mother, and in some places the protagonists have been deliberately "queered" as poet Jack Foley has pointed out. Italicized words in the final stanza are reading instructions to raise the voice an octave plus one note for that word. (Published by Serpentina Press as a chapbook in 2008 and by Aunt Lute Press in The Judy Grahn Reader, 2009).

ONE

That she could be on the street
in the rainy season, that my mother
could so easily be one of the butterflies
curled into a misery cocoon
under the bright plastic, color of a painted
suburban swimming pool, vivid blue shroud
heaped over the sleeping body
on the sidewalk
stained grey with water, stained with ice

that this could be her distressed dear face
struggling to the surface of one more day
among the million dollar apartments

butterflies die out when their habitat is destroyed

but it's all in the head,
it's mental,
isn't really real, isn't happening
not on our streets, not in this
civilized and monumental era
no, it isn't really happening that our streets
are crawling with bugs, with cocoons
with someone (showing signs of malnutrition
in his knobby elbows

I mean is *that* what it is?) leaning, bending down
shouting as though to voices talking to him from
under a car or maybe the license plate *is* broadcasting
maybe it's the government
propaganda
about the war.

no, it's all in our heads, it's mental

he isn't really bending and listening to voices
he isn't really walking around in a state of
malnutrition on our streets
listening to fenders
saluting the parking meters
among the million dollar apartments

TWO

So, Mickey and me were on the Sixth Floor Lockdown Ward B
until we were seventeen,
we were such great friends, we had so much to talk about
in spite of everything being so closed in, and
one day we escaped! yes, we ran out through the gate,
our gowns were flapping!
while no one was looking and we ran across the highway,
a broad white street with a bunch of trees and beautiful grass
in the center, we outran all the cars zigging and zagging
it was so much fun!
and we ran up to the biggest brownest greenest tree
and threw our arms
around the trunk, we just hugged and hugged that tree
giggling and yakking,
we loved it so much,
Mickey and me,
we hadn't seen one
for so long for years, we couldn't stop the hugging
and the yakking, and the loving
and the laughing
we stayed there for the longest time.

and then they came
and then they took us back.

So we were dancing gaily round a tree
and then confined again, constrained with drugs
and straps but not whipped as back in the 14th century
when England's Bedlam, originally
called *Bethlehem*, place meant to care for the down
and out became a house of torment for the "mad"—
"They," people said, "they don't work, they are
possessed and erratic,"
meaning: demonic, meaning bad

THREE

the mental health workers don't believe them
they think they are making it up, to shirk.
to avoid work.
it's all mental they say,
it's in their heads
they don't realize that if she thinks there are
bugs crawling on her skin, it's the same as if
there *are* bugs crawling on her skin

because it is, it is mental
and it's mental, so
if we think our streets
are crawling with the mentally ill

it's the same as if our streets
are crawling with the mentally ill

FOUR

when your parent has schizophrenia
the parent is like a, like a butterfly when they come out
but mostly what you see
is the cocoon, grey and spinning spinning
making a coat of protection
from *what* you wonder? but the cocoon
can't speak, it's all internal, separated
and preoccupied
you knock and knock, the child wanting
a response, realizing you can't get in
they can't get out
and just when you give up

here comes: a butterfly
so gorgeous, delicate and full of love
your heart opens up
and delight makes life seem real.
and probable and magic.
You stretch out your hand,
thinking you see a parent,

and it's gone
the cocoon returns, the inner spinning spinning
you can hear that much is going on in there
the munching of the larva, the devouring business
but it's secret
it's mental
you don't have access

sometimes you can see
that it's horrifying or dreadfully frightening
and you want to protect your parent
the vulnerability

sometimes you are just mad because no one
ever.   answers the door

well it isn't like any of that
what's the use trying to describe
what can't be known,
still, we have to try
and anyhow I am about a quarter butterfly
myself, and I know what that cocoon can feel like
though I've never had to live there all that long.
It's like being a porcupine with the quills turned
outside in.

and once, (or ok, more than once) I experienced the full blown
hallucination of horror, the distortion of senses that takes over.

This happened on a trip to the tropics, I was taking
Mefloquine for malaria prevention and hadn't read
the label that said if mental illness runs in your family
don't take this stuff.
It can make you crazy. and it did make me crazy,
the sensation was overwhelming, of paranoia,
the fear was a heart throbbing inner gigantic bug

the certainty I knew what was causing the fear, and
the absoluteness of how wrong I was,
though still picking up on something no one else could sense
and then the pervasive, invasive
inability to focus, to follow the plot of conversation
or procession.

I couldn't tell one end of the elephant from the other.
No wonder my mother couldn't tell what street we lived on
or how old we were if this is what preoccupied her life.

Worst were the physical hallucinations,
the revolting sensation of someone dear kissing me,
with lips that became writhing worms, long, thick, twisting,
lip-colored, way too alive. I could feel the worms
and I could *see* them from inside myself, where everything
is mental. I didn't tell anyone this because it was so
horrible, and I didn't want to be offensive. Just withdrew.
So that was a clue about my mother's mind and what she
went through all the time. What she contended with.
Inside herself. In that cocoon.

When I figured out the medication was the problem
and then remembered that malaria would wreck my liver
and possibly kill me:
"I don't care," I said, "I'd rather take the risk
than feel like *this* again"
even though it isn't *real*
it's only mental

FIVE

the sidewalks are the skin of the city, any city
has a grey skin like that and look! how it crawls
with bugs, people who are bugs! they are bugs!
in cocoons in the doorways, crawling on the skin
of the city and the city is panicky, pushing its hands
up and down its long grey arms, pushing and scratching
at the people who are bugs, trying to shake them off,
to squash them, make them go away

where shall they go?
to the jail, to the hospital
to the street

where shall they go?
to the jail, to the hospital
to the street

where shall they go?
to the jail, to the hospital
to the street

or hooligans may come in the night
where they sleep in their cardboard shacks
to mock and to beat
to mock and to beat
to mock and to beat

or even to set them on fire.
As during the Inquisition and its witch hunts
and during the continuing struggle afterwards
for a rational science
any expression of disparate energies was suspect,
epilepsy for example,
grounds for conviction of possession by evil spirits
women especially examined for the malady,
and diviners of all kinds arrested and tortured.
Even excessive joy was of the devil,
a symptom named "enthusiasm"[1]
On holidays crowds came to deride and
mock the antics of those afflicted.
Shock and awe the medication of choice,
everything from force feeding with cayenne pepper
to being thrown into a pit of snakes.

then came attempts to be more compassionate
so then came lunatic asylums, then drugs

1 as recorded in the bible of the witch hunters,
the *Malleus Malleficarum*.

then turned out on the street
free

    as

    bugs

SIX

my mom can't get treated, they say they have so many
so much worse off than her, so take her home.
But I know how this goes, I've seen it six times before,
it's elemental, she will get much worse and then
I can't get her in,
I can't get her back to the clinic
she won't go, she's too afraid, she's so afraid, and
then I must call for help and the authorities will come
and someone could get hurt,
they could hurt her, she could hurt somebody,
I'm thinking of Saturday, I turned my attention
to my niece for just one minute and during that time
my mother called 911,
next thing we knew the Tact Squad at the door

forcing their way in with rifles and those looks,
so departmental.
She said he was murdering us all,
"No," I told them, "it's her illness." And so glad she didn't
threaten them, they didn't shoot her.

And then taking her to the clinic
I don't need to hear a lecture on how much worse off
the others are, out there in the streets.

She's as worse off as she needs to be to get the treatment
if only they would believe me, I am the daughter,

I am her primary caretaker,
as I have been most of my life,
so I know, who knows her better than I?

they are afraid, so afraid, so irrationally afraid

SEVEN

they hallucinate, they think they see a threat where there is none

as when the young man suffered an emotional breakdown
and stood in an empty theater
with a knife, his girlfriend called the police for help
and they shot him forty eight times shot forty eight times shot forty eight times
forty eight times shot forty eight times shot forty eight times
they thought they saw Godzilla, giant dark crazy devil axis of evil

they thought they saw the great satan, yes that was surely him,
eating the entire city, sticking all the downtown buildings
into his gigantic mouth
(he's the mother of all bugs)

And his mother. She sued the hell out of them.
(and so they said they got some training)

What if we don't need to choose
between lockdown asylums and the streets
what if we create a geography of disparate spirits?
what if space were set aside for behaviors like these:

dance on one leg, sing for hours off key,
scream and roll around,
hold your breath, accuse the universe of crimes
listen to essential messages from bees

rock all day pace all night
recognize strangers but not your family
pound your furies into the stalwart bodies of trees
say the weirdest ideas right out loud, fly into a cloud,
no need to fear your hysteria will bring chains
or a ring of whitecoat people terrified of being sued,
or a ring of bluecoat people terrified. of worse than death.
and shooting. you.   shooting.   you.

EIGHT

think what a butterfly does to our life
that's elemental

there is nothing substantial about a butterfly
it doesn't feed you or give you a bed
it doesn't remember what street we live on or how old you are
There is nothing about a butterfly we would want
to take to the insurance adjustor, nothing incremental.

But think what a butterfly gives us
of delight, think what surprise in that flutter of life
and how amazing the colors, who would ever have imagined
such combinations as a butterfly takes for granted
in its short display of light play
and that sacramental face, those sensitive antennae
connecting to our inner eyes.

There are dances, notions and inspirations
we can't know except for butterflies

that we can't know when there are no butterflies
when life is detrimental
and when the habitat, the habitat of butterflies

is so destroyed
what is the covenant
we must have with butterflies.

not that I'm really talking about butterflies,
not that they aren't dangerous at times
and crawl from their cocoons onto an entirely different
landscape than any we can imagine

remember my mother threw an iron into my face
when I was four; who knows what monster she saw,
some reports from deep in those cocoons tell us
their babies turn into satan or a hairy watermelon
or God gives them specific instructions from His boombox
and so they drop him out the window or into the Bay or run over her,
that baby, that writhing bucket of snakes.

a mother may try to kill you in a number of ways.
and then there were those kittens unexpectedly dying,
my father and I sobbing, she so still with no expression on her face.
My mother was willful, once at the hospital for a routine physical
the confident doctor insisted on giving her an EKG
she didn't want, so she said no, (her no is a no)
he said ho ho ho
and hooked her up anyhow
as soon as she was alone she shredded the connections,
five thousand dollars damage, and innocence, whimsical,
let's hear how "she's so sweet"

now imagine being her daughter or her son, trying to hold
onto your sense of balance, your space, your clothes, your kittens . . .
your friends and the minor matter of lunch and dinner

and ferocious fear . . . that someone will come and take her away . . .
or that they won't . . . or that they will . . . or that they won't . . .
and then they don't.   So you don't have   exactly a mother,
you're left with sort of a child. Occasionally, wild.

and you don't speak about this, as there is no one to hear you

Everyone thinks schizophrenic means helpless and locked up for life
but lo! there are a lot of functional folks with the illness and they have
jobs and families, some have children, just imagine being five or nine and
taking care of the parent with the condition no one can talk about or think about,
that comes and goes, because he is mostly stable, except for episodes,

and meantime everyone thinks he is so sweet, they tell you,
they rather insistently tell you,
    "Your father is so sweet," and you are thinking
"yes, he has that blazing open-sky sweetness
            of butterflies," or you are thinking,
"why does everyone say that
except his children?"

those children secretly, obsessively scurrying from one definition
of sanity to another, trying to sort. Knowing

it's like being from an unknown country, always astonished
at everything everyone does, because after a while it all seems
like cocoon life to you, it all seems equally irrational,
this may give you quite a sense of humor
and people will say that you are a bit quirky, even fay.
you won't have an answer for this.   you won't say.

NINE

They are demented and so
are likely to kill the children
or otherwise terrify them.

You spend your days, in uniform,
saluting parking meters on Mission Street.
sent back for a third time, a third deploymental decision
omygodomygod my ticket is up
soldier you were given instructions to fire upon civilians
to protect yourself

how now will you live with this
how *will* you protect yourself? from this:
given amphetamines to keep you up up up
til you can't tell friend from foe,
instructed to kill whatever comes near

your vulnerable lethal humbug vehicle
how now will you exist with these ghosts
how *will* you protect yourself
from those curled little lumps staining the backseat
(after you come back down)

you could smell their stillness when the noise settled
in back of the bloody windshield
what shield will protect the tender eye of your memory
from child, student, old man, pregnant woman
terrified driver trying to back up the car

what *will* protect you from the screaming mothers
how now will you live with these nightmare memories
of the car that goddammit didn't blow up even after you shot
everyone in it

the country sends you like bad thoughts from its house of bugs
all dressed up in the pretty camouflage
and not quite enough exoskeleton armors
eyes wrapped in the dark rhomboid lenses
bugged, bugged, bugged, we are all bugged
as the arrogant cocoons in such big white houses, plotting
and frothing, bugging everyone,
listening to God broadcast from little black boxes
the end of his regime

urging the people to be
flag-wavingly sentimental
seeking purification in self fulfilling
delusions of armageddon

as the fundamental hallucinations of
virgins, angels and martyrs
dancing on the heads of missiles
a thousand times the numbers required
for annihilation of the lovely little blue planet
to get to states of transmogrification
for true believers where nothing is mental
it's all moral

allegedly, but really more loyal, so
augmentally regimental
as millionbillionaire men of powerful super nation
vent upon whole peoples

being so instrumental

you could be anyone's son, you could be
my mother, wrapped in a blue room, or
complementally, she could be me
and you, the soldier, the one who joined because

you wanted to rescue someone, or felt you had no better choices
your father was a soldier and this is a caste system
you had no idea it would be like this, you only wanted to grow up
you didn't know you would want to kill everything

on a very particular singular cocoon-feeling day

blown out of your mind with grief
seeing your friends melt to just bloody bones
and you not even scraped
(and you as far as anyone can get from home)

you didn't know your buddies would go mad with bloodlust
and rape you
in the fog of butterflies
whose habitat has been destroyed

and so you will live on the *street*, babe
you will live on the street like a *holy man*
owning nothing but your beard and the visible *pinkscabs*
eating away your hands like infectious *beetles*
and your eyes like ponds in a meadow of *nowhere*
    as you feed the pigeons the last of your trust in *anyone*
       owning no gas guzzling cars no *property*
          nothing that calls for AK Kalashnikov to guard the pearly *gates of*
            owing nobody *nothing*
and so they will call you that strange and *traveling word:*

that word of prophets, murderers, and *survivors*
that word that sets you apart from them that *accomplish* things:

craaaaazy

they will call YOU   *craaazy*

CROSSING (2016)

"Crossing" will be part of The Queen of Cups, *my third book-length poem tracing Helen of Troy back in time to goddess Inanna of Sumer, and forward in time to Helena of the Gnostic writings. Helena's mythological journey includes status as both a creation goddess, and an embodied human, who during the time of the life of Jesus was a prostitute in a brothel at Tyre, from which she was rescued by the magician Simon Magus. Whether in reality or story, Mary Magdalen may have known her. The two of them, and two additional goddess voices, Ma, and Whirling, participate in this polyvocal poem. "Oracle," a diviner who sees into both past and future, serves as moderator for the story-telling these mythic characters share, sitting around a pond, at the "conference" called for them by "the Queen of Cups."*

ONE

Oracle:

Oracle here, water diviner
transmitting for the Queen of Cups,
who is present in the form of a pond
and who has asked four prominent deities
to a three day conference.
They have gathered around her dark bright water
to share their stories.
Tonight they speak to us
on the subject of transformation,
at which they are all experienced.

Before we get to them,
first I'd like
to tell you a bit about my own transits in my
day job as midwife or boatman crossing
others through the tunnel of life.
Example one, imagine a boatload of teenagers
each needing initiation, and me rowing them
across the hazardous passage.
They are giggling, pushing and leaning on each other
no idea where the other side is,
no notion who of them will grow all the way up or old
who will crash against a wall of cease, whose disease
will turn into a good luck charm,
who will find love or not
even try, who will tie the ropes of connection
(making every passage possible).
For now I row them, give them good will,
my good strong arms, as much attention
as I can.
Example two, Tuesdays and Thursdays I serve

a different population (of whom I have grown fond)
though nevertheless am rowing
on the same long pond:

One gives up knitting
another gives away his money
a third takes up biting and spitting

Sinking alone, or buoyed by daughters
every week I row them further
across silent waters

Night and day change places
mysterious as existence
names dissolve, then faces

Identity slides off like clothing
time eats itself to nothing
some forget where they are going

Some fall off balance
others never lose their bearings
act as group compass

Who will be which, ever
unpredictable as weather—
mysterious as existence.

And now to the goddesses, each with a moment
in her life of complete transformation.
We begin with an important weekend for Magdalen
(visionary of the Christians).

TWO

Magda:

But if you're going to go
dying on your tree
don't forget to come
back to me, give me this

Send me a cloud of birds
messages of mist
and dreams, dreams I can
remember, vivid and real
dreams I can tell

How we used to go strolling
down along the beach
to watch the early morning light
walk upon the water
That's you, I would say, *that's your spell*

As we were talking
you would reach for my hand
you know I can't *stand*
not to see you again
not to feel your body near
not to hear your voice

But I need the choice
not to follow your pain
I want to stay here
for as long as I can
I don't yet want to cross
to wherever you are

Wasn't it bad enough
I had to watch you
meet your nails
wasn't it bitter enough
I had to solace others
over your travails

Wasn't it sad enough
I had to accompany your mother
while we washed you
the prescribed number of times
the prescribed prayers and herbs
I, who never prescribed anything
except you and your words

Don't forget to come back again
don't forget to give me the kiss
to last a lifetime
if you're going to go dying
on your cross
at least toss me a lifeline
don't forget to come back to me
don't just leave me, give me this

THREE

   Oracle:

She reported what she had seen
and heard to the apostles, who could
hardly believe her at first.
Magdalen's message was that
something lives over on the other side
that sends us love (and further that these forms

we occupy just now, are not the only ones).
Magdalen's message was received; at first her heart
was golden. Chastity, fidelity, obedience
became her habits.
Yet in the centuries after, she was so degraded,
disregarded, all the credit given to the vision
rather than the visionary, just as people
in a township drink the water every day
and don't recall the engineer who found
the aquifer and dug the well . . . yet worse, imagine
hatred for the engineer, calling him a thief . . .
as Magdalen could tell you, those who believe
in paradise believe also in its opposite,
and those who love sacrifice love suffering,
then long ceaselessly for comfort.

Let's turn now to a goddess with a different
philosophy. One whose adventures here on earth
inevitably include rising
and falling, and rising
and falling . . .

FOUR

   Helena:

When the moon had set in the west
he came into my little room,
he came into my room where the bed
was sturdy-made for many men in turn
to enter in, but he, the magician,
waited until the moon had set in the west
to come into my little room.

"What do you like?" I asked, "what do you like best?"
"Your mouth is sweet," he said, "your words, your voice
is lovely, spills like honey from a honeycake—
your hands," he said, "are beautiful as well."
"Oh no," I laughed, "my hands are rough from two years
in the dye troughs." "Let's put some cream on them,"
he said and rubbed my fingers with the moisturizer
kept nearby to help my poor cunny through its busiest days.

We sat together on the bed.
"What do you like?" I asked again, then
"What are you doing here?"
He was looking into my eyes.
"What are *you* doing here?" he answered.
Well I thought, he only wants to talk,
a middle aged man with me, barely twenty,
one of those lonely ones who doesn't
have the stuff, but has the money.

His lips brushed my face, which jumped back.
"I do not kiss," I said, "a kiss is for a troth,
a promise of fidelity." I was sure he knew this.
"Tell me about your dreams," he said. "Do you
have visions of the future?"
"Yes," I said, "I know which foot is on the step,
whose fist is pounding at my door.
And more, I knew when my mother was dying,
I know when the Romans are off to the next war,
and more, I feel I've lived before."

"You have," he said, "I'll tell you about that in a while.
How do you get to states of deepest knowing?"
He had pulled back my robe to look at my breasts,
the nipples staring out like curious faces.
"This is my most pressing question, do you ever

feel as though you're flying? Do you space travel?
How does this happen? If you can tell me
we can dance together for a long time."

"It's a special kind of sex," I said, opening my thighs.
I showed him my clitoris, its head hard as a plum.
"It's this wand," I said, "let's wave it." Rubbing
slow at first, then faster, looking into his eyes,
wondering what he meant by "dance,"
my heart turning into a drum.
And then in front of him, I went into a trance.

He followed me over, we stayed a long while,
and I saw us under a huge tree with crowds
of people breathing in our every word or stance.
Nothing about it felt strange, and when we awoke
I knew he would buy my freedom and I would go with him,
around the countryside where we were seen as gods,
that everything about my life, and his, had changed.

FIVE

    Oracle:

So Helena hooked up with the magician
Simon, who would morph gradually into a scientist.
Every two thousand year-long eon
the iconic man is claimed by Helen for her own.
She loved the bull in the age of Taurus, the shepherd king in
the age of Aries the ram, and the magician turned scientist
in the age of Pisces.
Next will come the waterman.

Wait! This just in from Pen, aka Penthesilea,
the Amazon warrior who fought for Helen
in the battle at Troy. Go ahead Pen!

Pen:

First of all I need to say that if you
want to fly, two women are the way to go.
Two triangles make a pair of wings.
But I know that won't happen, to her
I am the one in her field of defense,
never the one in the palace,
never the one stretched out beside Her,
naked and trembling
with my heart in her hand. If I could get
inside her, foot to head I'd merge
all the way under that beautiful skin
and never come out again.

Oracle:

All right, thanks for that report.
Such a sweet story, isn't it? The beauty mired
in a brothel, rescued by the magic man, an amazing
romance, erotic and spiritual both at once.

Here's what happened after the age of
Helena and Simon, gods of wisdom.
As I told you
he became a scientist and she, astonishingly,
the muse of capital. He became boundless curiosity
yoked to acquisition. She became desire itself,
made musky slippery with money.

Bound only to production and trade, She split
away from nature and the psyche. She became the sexy
itch that makes you want to go shopping, the wide net
sucking everybody in.
Find something beautiful, intriguing, easy to take home,
and ultimately unfulfilling as a very flirtatious
very ungiving lover.

He became inventor of endless objects; she became
the saleswoman soliciting salivation, yet leading
to the adulation of the "most beautiful" of women at expense
of all the others. Boundless punishment for absence of perfection,
as she ended blamed for every excess of her ages.
(Scorned by Magdalen's followers, Helena went secular.)

Eventually the lovely trance receded; he became a crass materialist
pawing at the breast of nature, sticking his hands
into her every cornucopian basket, while praying "more more more."
And Helena nearly disappeared, became "I want it" as well as freedom,
blessed liberty but also license for devouring. That needed
to change as people realized the values "enticement" and "comfort"
weren't such great ones after all.

Shhhhh! Don't say anything more bad about her!
Haven't you seen her with her torch of freedom?
Or in her butterfly form, hovering over children
as an angel of protection?
Venus is goddess of true value.
She wants only to love you.

Our next speaker, beloved of animists,
may or may not confirm.

SIX

Ma:

Black ocean, night sky a garment of flowers,
performing their dances in axial turns.
On earth, mass migration is the new normal,
rippling the robe of life, everyone on the run,

running, twisting from the great devour.
Leaving tent cities, boats capsized, animal eyes
of wonder at increase of trauma,
not knowing exactly how now to be wise.

On earth elite humans hide in their towers,
ordinary folks take a strange faith in guns,
as chemicals, petroleum, metal, fuel turmoil,
smaller-eyed beings fall silent of tongue.

Me I am Ma, their eons my hours,
scope of My life full of minor turns.
I prevent suffering by making things formal,
more or less steady, more or less fun.

I prevent suffering by balancing, showers
with sunlight, laws of my nature to shelter the land.
Take only as much as you need, think of "ours"
and give back whenever you can.

Once in a while a disruption of powers—
usually collision of meteor runs—
this time and to their own conscious horror,
this time the grandiose tiniest of ones

speeded up, unwrapped My robe of all flowers,
shut down their precious connections to being,
with inflated sense of importance and power,
they, who are tinier to Me than microbes to them.

For three of My days they've been planters and plowers,
given the bounty to burst at their seams.
I wish them a solace in midst of their sorrow,
connections to whole-ness, the hearts of all beings.

No one is ever that far from my bower,
even if all I can give you is calm.
A bit of compassion this current cross-over,
no one is ever that far from my arms.

Me, I am Ma, the cup and the ladle;
fruits of all looms and turns of the sun.
Me, I am Ma, both stitcher and cradle.
My robe is eternal, never will be done.

How to approach Me? First thing, humility;
secondly, service to whatever is alive.
Unconditional love requires permeability,
surrender the ego, have faith I'll arrive.

SEVEN

Oracle:

Ma, thank you. Ma covers a lot of territory. Our last
speaker is more intently focused.
The robe of life lies lightly on the desert floor
which heats up faster because the rocks are bare.
Whirlwind sucks up the heated ground air

and spins it into the sky in exchange
for cooler, downward driven air, clever, hey?
And welcome relief for cricket, toad, and lizard
mothers and fathers living there.

Whirlwinds are frequent and local.
As a whirlwind Whirling has accompanied some of the other
deities in their sagas, but she also has a tornado life of her own
most recently on US Midwest plains, as conveyer of a certain
yellow brick road. Cold air clashing with hot
drives her formation.
Now let's hear what the ferocious and mysteriously
quixotic storm tornado can do.

Whirling is not so much an identity
as an event, a confluence happening
at latitude and longitude such and such,
in precinct X, time, date, location code *thus*.
Life span relatively succinct.
And couldn't this be said of any of us?

Goddess Whirling is accompanied
by her companion dog Boot, with drum and vocals.

EIGHT

Whirling: Boot:

Whirl up, wind.
Be my breath of speech.   spin, spin
Tell what needs to happen
what is out of reach.

Hot/cold round
from cloud emotions
funnel snakes down.   spin.spin.spin.
Paradox in motion.

Whirl out, world,
tunnel of suction   eat, eat
churns in action
at this junction

Construction dissembles,
blown from within.   eat eat eat. eat eat
Function stumbles,
Losing rhythm.

Whirl in, rain.
Flood plains. Wash
structural sins. Tears for pain
of loss, death I've caused.   sing, sing, sing

Please recall
safely set down
herd of cows,
and babe unharmed.

Reset plan: sing, sing
rewrite instructions,
double check directions,
begin again.

Whirl up, change,
fresh theories, maps,   cross, cross
habitat and range,
preserve that.

Fix habits,   cross cross cross
sweep in tenderness,
adjust practices, keep
tending-in-distress.

Whirl on, Earth
Earth, whirl on.
Thanks for the invitation,   spin. spin. spin.
more than worth it.

Let me know
Will you? Whenever you
need me to turn into
myself for you, again.   spin, spin

NINE

    Oracle:

You've now heard our experts. All go forward
into the eon; their voices intensify. Ma's robe
continues to shred, and change becomes the theme.
Helena's next love will be Aquarius, the Water-bearing One,
science with full arc of emotions,
kindly, likes to help others, can be very shy and
intellectual, always tells the truth, but easily
diverted and even subject to addictions;
She will need to hold strong boundaries,
especially with the world in flux.

What do I see?
There are new hybrid species every day,
crowds of rich young people trading places
with the poor, gleefully experimenting

with community and festivals that celebrate
survival here on earth; old folks dedicating
the last twenty years of life to service, thousands
of whole towns adopting groups of beings in transit,
or tracts of land and water to care for and preserve.
So many prisons now converted to esteemed places
of meditation and recuperation from the fray.

Work is no longer adulated, the term is "serve"
instead; identity has nearly disappeared,
for instance five of my friends transitioning
from one gender to another or to more than one,
while two who did are now transferring back (and three
became another species altogether). Black and white
not viable categories. Spectrum of creativity matters more
than anything 'rich' or 'poor.' I myself no longer
know which names to call myself. Next
time we'll tell you what we think this means.

BIOGRAPHICAL NOTE

Judy Grahn is an internationally known poet, writer, and social theorist. Her poetry collections include *Edward the Dyke and Other Poems* (1971), *She Who* (1977), *The Work of a Common Woman* (1978), *The Queen of Swords* (1987), and *love belongs to those who do the feeling* (2008), among others. In addition to poetry, Grahn's nonfiction explores history, mythology and cultural theory. In *Another Mother Tongue: Gay Words, Gay Worlds* (1984) she explores queer meanings, while *The Highest Apple: Sappho and the Lesbian Poetic Tradition* (1985) focuses on the ways poetry has served as a vehicle for establishing a lesbian literary tradition. Her novel, *Mundane's World* (1988), constructs an imagined world centered around women's spiritual and social practices. In 2009, *The Judy Grahn Reader*, representing all phases of Grahn's writing career, was published by Aunt Lute Books.

Her work has won numerous awards and honors, including an American Book Review Award, two American Book Awards, the American Library Association Stonewall Book Award, the Bill Whitehead Award for Lifetime Achievement, the Golden Crown Lifetime Achievement in Lesbian Letters Award, the Fred Cody Award for Lifetime Achievement in Literature and Community Service from the Northern California Book Reviewers Association, a Founding Foremothers of Women's Spirituality Award, two Lambda Literary Awards, and a Pioneer Gay Writer Award from Outlook in 1989. She was Lifetime Achievement Grand Marshall of the San Francisco Gay Pride Parade in 2014. In 1999, her book *Another Mother Tongue* served as the major theme of the Seattle Gay Pride Parade. In 1996 the Publishing Triangle, an association of lesbians and gay men in publishing, established an award in her name: The Judy Grahn Award, recognizing the best nonfiction book of the year.

Judy Grahn is currently Associated Distinguished Professor, Integral and Transpersonal Psychology, California Institute of Integral Studies in San Francisco, where in the 1990s she earned her PhD in Integral Studies. She served as co-director for an MA program in Women's Spirituality for thirteen years, and for an MFA in Creative Inquiry for five years. She does several public readings and presentations a year, and teaches classes in writing and women's literature.

CPSIA information can be obtained
at www.ICGtesting.com
Printed in the USA
BVOW08s1156090717
488800BV00002B/4/P